HOLOGLYPHS II

Afterlight

HOLOGLYPHS II
Afterlight

A collection of poems

by

S. K. YEATTS

Adelaide Books
New York / Lisbon
2021

HOLOGLYPHS II

Afterlight

holo   noun \hō-lə-\ or \hol\ whole; entire; complete

glyph   noun \glif\ symbol or image that conveys information nonverbally

Hologlyph \hō-lə, glif\ whole image

HOLOGLYPHS II

Afterlight

A collection of poems

By S. K. Yeatts

Copyright © by Stan K. Yeatts

Cover design © 2021 Stan K. Yeatts

Published by Adelaide Books, New York / Lisbon
adelaidebooks.org

Editor-in-Chief
Stevan V. Nikolic

All rights reserved. No part of this book may be reproduced in any manner whatsoever without written permission from the author except in the case of brief quotations embodied in critical articles and reviews.

For any information, please address Adelaide Books
at info@adelaidebooks.org
or write to:
Adelaide Books
244 Fifth Ave. Suite D27
New York, NY, 10001

ISBN: 978-1-955196-56-7

Contents

2:22 a.m.	13
60	14
762 AD	15
Afterlife	16
After Reading a John Ashbery Poem on a Terrace Outside Castellina in Chianti	17
At Chaco Canyon	18
At Cologny II	19
At Rocca di Asolo	20
At Santa Maria degli Angeli e dei Martiri	21
At the Funeral	22
At Villa Eyrie	23
Aural Silhouettes	24
Autumn Eventually Came	25
Awakening at Dusk	26
Azrael	27
Banshee	28
Bell of Geese	29
Benediction	30
Berlin – October	31
Between	32

Between Us – The Small Slow Ghosts	33
Beyond the Blue Cliff	34
Borrowed	42
Cempasúchitl	43
Churches are Empty	44
Closing	45
Coming Night at Mathais Gardens	46
Cornfields and Graves	47
Corona – 1947	48
Cuckoo at Deià	49
Darkness Across the West	50
Death Poem	51
Déjà vu III	52
Desvelado	53
Dreamers	54
Driving at Night	55
Eikon	56
Eikon II	57
End of Days III	58
End of Evening	59
Enlightenment	60
Enlightenment II	61
Enso	62
Entangled	63
Evensong	64
Exile	65
Face in Evening Clouds	66
Fall	67

Faux	68
First and Only	69
Forecast	70
Foreshadowing for a Desert Night	71
Fortune	72
Garden of White Clouds	73
Ghost Dance	74
Ghost House II	75
Ghosts	77
Glass Angels	78
Going Down	79
Hearing a Clock Somewhere Down the Hall	80
Hegira	81
I Have Seen you in the Darkening Garden	82
Icon	83
Irrational Numbers	84
Isle of the Dead	85
Kyrie for the End of Spring	86
Lacrimosa	87
Late October	89
Listening to a Crow at Lake Biwa	90
Long Count	91
Los Endos	92
Lost Image	93
Lure	94
Magdalene	95
Mallorca - Autumn	96
Mary in the Night Room	97

Masque	99
Mendocino 1979	100
Metaphysical	101
Meteor Fall over the San Juan Mountains	102
Ministry	103
Mnemonic	104
Moon and Star Over Île de la Cité	105
Morning at St. Magdalena	106
New York Evening – Autumn 1984	107
Nightscape	108
Nineteen Pictures from an Exhibition	109
Nocturne	119
Oracle	120
Oubliette	122
Out of Alfacar	123
Pentimento	124
Plight and Premonition	126
Prayer After the Canon	127
Predator	128
Premonition	129
Quincunx	130
Realization	131
Reconsidered on Night Streets Around Piazza Navona	132
Red Wing Blackbirds at Jalama Beach	133
Revelation	134
Setting a Clock	135
Shadows at the Harbor	136
Simulation	137

Small Bridges	138
Snow Garden	139
Snow in the Desert	140
Sound Without Fury	141
Spiegel im Spiegel	142
Storm	143
Sunset Tint	145
Swans at Vitznau	147
Ten Views of a Moment	148
Tenebrae	150
Terrace	151
Theater of Man	152
Three Figures at Blue Mesa	153
Three Trios	154
Three Views of the Evening	169
To a Minor 21st Century Poet	172
Traveling in the Mountains	173
Tuscan Dusk	174
Union Station – 10 p.m.	175
Valle di Cadore	176
Vespers	177
When it is Time	178
Whispered in the Evening	179
Winter Garden	180
Winter Morning	181
Zen and Chan Redux	182

2:22 a.m.

I have noticed the clock at 2:22 before –
Something repeated against sleeping silvered windows.

There was no one on the empty streets.
Everything was held in place by not looking.
It was not a shadow down the dark hall of Autumn,
Or some near waking –
It was only luminous remainders of our unwilling return.

Before –
Spirals of ravens traced Mandelbrot-eternities over miles of golden larch.
It could have been the end,
Or just the end of Summer.

A few clouds twisted into chalk equations of black-poppy skies.
It was not a shadow down the dark hall of Autumn,
Or some pale found-light –
It was only scrawled numerals written in vapor -
Passing memories of wind and night.

Motionless,
Everything was rushing by,
Held in place by not looking:
A coincidence of purpose -
A premonition of aligned hours beyond a single life.

After –
Perhaps it was the end of Summer,
Some near-waking of found light,
Or our shadows down the dark hall of Autumn -

Coming again at 2:22 to sleeping silvered windows.

60

Under a cold scripture of closing heavens,
I could not wait for you.

In the luminous dust of hill towns,
You walked dark streets of Spain –
An abstract figure in Siguirya of poems.

In anticipation of yesterday,
Summers ran out.

It was at the edge of balance,
And a great height from the terrace of memory,
Where I could only see you from outside the illusion –
Shadows of what would come and what had long been completed.

Under a cold scripture of heavens,
Everything was closing.
And I could not wait for you.

762 AD

Night falls in apricot blossoms,
Where snow will come again.

After we left,
Dusk brushed your cold hair
In a scent of silver winter.

Afterlife

In early light before the dark sails of summer,
The garden filled with a wind of iris in a last cold breath of spring,

From this remote village,
Hours flew in owls of sleep,
As a mausoleum of stars slowly opened around some remaining time.

It is your empty hands
That keep me here.

After Reading a John Ashbery Poem on a Terrace Outside Castellina in Chianti

After reading a John Ashbery poem on a terrace outside Castellina in Chianti,
She said: "...*L'Imperatore è nudo*...".

The summer was over,
And Bougainvillea leaves littered the garden path in phrases of red light.

I said nothing,
And kept listening to a pale sparrow out in the darkening vineyard.

At Chaco Canyon

Our twilight
Echoed on the stone stairs of summer,
Where one August,
We walked all the way to the Jackson Staircase
Under a distant warning of storm light.

It was a Chronos of wind following –
Voices from rocks – an inland tourniquet and failing turquoise skies –
A long silence of afternoons closing in.

And even with our water running out,
Our ankles held, and we return to the charade of the living –
Where among these perfect ruins,
We sensed a fragile calendar of eternity – only continuing -

Held in some desire to be remembered -
Held in some Planck-length of love.

At Cologny II

Old poplars smoldered auric fires of October
Where we walked by shadowed villas,
In long echoes of becoming.

How lovely are these days:
Ghosts - Never arriving or leaving,
Waiting above the lake
With the voices of deliverance and sorrow.

It is said,
The dead are never gone.

From a small boat on Leman,
Byron and Shelley continue to hear Alpen horns
Somewhere south toward Mont Blanc,
As clear and timeless as the evening star.

At Rocca di Asolo

Above Asolo in a remainder of olive groves,
Figures of cypress and Calendula
Painted the way the evening.

Stone pools calmed fallen histories
Beyond our time.

Along the piazza,
Paper and tin stars smoked over blue murmur of Atlas trees.

Below these hills,
Puzzled fields in a thousand-shades of *Verde Candeias*
Sketched an abstract afternoon
All the way to the Isola di San Michele.

Cathedral bells began a long arc
Into aural landscapes of whispered white fire,
And senescence of unfinished oeuvres -
Offering nothing.

From the distances of now,
Grey terns in black caps circled these battlement walls
In September's great waiting.

We could not finish what we had intended.
There was nothing to do.

It was a remainder of olive groves
And a not yet recalled end of days -
Painting the way to evening.

At Santa Maria degli Angeli e dei Martiri

A bridge of stone heavens
Blocks the crossing of a life.

Years collapse into future architectures of return,
As carved eyes of martyr's stare into the void,
From the sundials of Santa Maria degli Angeli

It was a foreshadowing of atonal choirs –
A white chant of footsteps or rain,
Wearing away an apparition of angels,
And votive ghosts of finished fire for the beloved.

Here at solstice,
In the high fields before fall,
Without intent, herds graze in a cacophony of bells and confused light.

On cathedral spires,
A few ravens waited in the failing light -
Mocking a music of the spheres.

At the Funeral
<Alla Ricerca del Temps Perdito>

At the funeral,
A cold sign of stars
Circled the virgin's pale brow
In ice and some shallow nimbus of all we might have been.

Here, before winter –
After a priest's hollow words,
It was a cold sign of stars -
And alone together,
From all these great distances,
We stepped out to silent fields,
Accepting a final blessing and red eulogies of quiet rustling maples.

At Villa Eyrie

Cassia trees sighed in a silver wind.

Light-years of Rhododendrons
Bloomed again beyond our few lives.

A cerise sash of stars calmed a lack of accomplishment.
An empty path lead to dawn.

Aural Silhouettes

Songs of a blackbird
Aged in texts of yellow Larch.

A line of fields became dark,
As light-years of wonder
Littered twilight with rippling voices of leaves:

Prayer flags for the dead.

Autumn Eventually Came

Autumn eventually came.

Looking into nothing –
Sirens of coyotes echoed over these canyons,
From a series of cold nights:
Vespers of unfinished scores and nothing more.

Across an aging light,
Too soon -
The soft glow faded from your face:
Prisoners waiting for dawn
In this little space of waking -
A fallen stain of shadows sweeping the unkempt garden.

In a lost grace of the moment as everything began again,
Looking into nothing –
Too soon,
It was a series of cold night –
It was a siren of unfinished scores -
It was a premonition of returning old age,
And the Buddha's fabricated words -
Where the glow faded,
And Autumn eventually came.

Awakening at Dusk

Following evening's wandering light,
Tinted winds washed rosary colors
From the transept at St. Johann's.
Distant choirs painted aural silhouettes
On cold canvas of closed cloisters.

We had heard this before.

A nimbus of heavens
Arced over silver geese in some slow compass of fire.
Perhaps winter would come again.

Out of aging towers,
Exact shadows of clocks darkened uncertain hours:
Old hands circling the smooth throat of night
Where we could not speak.

Awakening at dusk,
It was residual echoes in flickered feet
Wearing down stones of the cathedral nave.
It was final ghosts of October chrysanthemums
In fallen colors at St. Johann's.
It was a score of moments
And lost directions to morning.

Following evening's wandering light,
Nomadic hours counted steps back to our silence,
As winter would come again in a glittered nimbus of mapless heavens:
Old hands circling the throat of night
Where we could not speak.

Azrael
<small><Valami></small>

This ruin of evening
Slips through unsteady hands.

Years after our death,
Poppies danced in returning shadows
And filled the plaza with blood of the setting sun.

Directionless,
Our voice will come again like a cold wind at open doors.

In a stain of the eternal return –
Without permission -
We are our Bardo light.

Banshee

While under some false notion of ghosts,
I am not a Paul Celan to your Ivan Goll,
As you always lived beyond our fragile light.

To observe is not to command,
As you were long overthrown by the spirits you kept.

The night remains quite wild
With or without anyone's permission.

North America, Greece – It makes no difference.

It will be light soon,
But it is far too late to start paying attention at this point.

Bell of Geese
        <For Ann Miller>

And you were a blue silence at the end of summer,
Waiting in the held breath of what are called dreams.

After your amber day,
Prayers and votive candles continued,
As intent rose over achievement.

In an unfinished text,
Along clear streets of September
Words of fire declined into dust of closed books,
Where autumn's white voices would never come again.

Over the Texas town –
The empty morning came in bells and aerial shadows of geese.

Rest. Prepare for sleep.
Not yet, and always,
It will be the held breath of this amber day,
Under a requiem of bells and geese.

It was only a day,
And you were a blue silence at the end of summer.

Benediction

A yellow Tanager sings a *Lux Aeterna*
In darkening Norwegian spruce without any consequence.

Your eyes blur these hills in glaucoma of valerian and smoke:
A coming ransom of wind and falling leaves,
In defiance of conventional reason.

Around our heads,
Stars formed distant wreaths of bright marigolds -
It was a zodiac of the bygone summers we could never regain.

The gates were closing,
And beyond reason in the last titian light,
The guards allowed us to pass.

Berlin – October

After the gala dinner,
Along white winds of fall,
Suppressed color of flags rippled over darkened streets
From Karl-Liebknecht-strasse to Dircksenstrabe.

There was a spotlight of moon,
Sweeping for fugitive grackles in clock-hands of twisted trees.

Under distractions of achivement,
I walked back to the hotel -
A ghost among apparitions of men.

Between

Whether noticed or not,
All afternoon it was the same cloud
Holding a static motion –
Particles in waves of ocean-skies,
Proving nothing.

All afternoon,
Fates remain unsealed,
And I waited by my open gate –

But still you did not come.

Between Us – The Small Slow Ghosts

Waiting for yesterday,
Stones, wheat and poppies
Pieced together a passing afternoon -
Between us, the small slow ghosts.

From summer's sleep of olive oceans,
We came out to sea-greens of wind and swaying zebra-grass
But there was nothing to say.

Under aerial fields of Ruhnau-blue air,
It was cathartic murals of where we once stood -
And where we could have been.

Cartographs of stars began to appear
Over charts of darkening worlds.
Everything stood still as the light moved on.

Waiting for yesterday,
We came out to pieces of afternoon,
And lovely ruins of where we once stood.

Between us, the small slow ghosts.

Beyond the Blue Cliff

<After the Chan Traditions of Umon, Engo and Setcho>

Case 101

<Rikyu Sweeps the Garden Path>

Sky's Introduction

To openly ask or answer is like attempting to count stars on one hand.
Who would ever do this?
See the following.

Main Subject

After an overnight storm,
A monk found Rikyu in the garden and asked: Is the world out there, or inside us? Rikyu did not answer and continued to sweep the garden path.
On getting no reply, the monk addressed Rikyu again with the same question (thinking the old master did not hear him). Rikyu stopped sweeping and handed the broom to the monk – saying: Not out there. Not in here. The path needs sweeping.

Sky's Commentary

Neither inside nor outside.
Too large to find - too small to hide.
What a shame, Old Rikyu gave the broom away too quickly when there was so much left to sweep.

Sky's Verse

Cherry flowers or snow.
To ask about this misses the season.
Sweeping everything clear:

The garden is nowhere to be found.
Clouds in mountains - Mountains in clouds.

Rinpoche's Teishō

Between broom and path, dust grows thick. After the storm,
Wind brings a sound of sweeping.

Case 102

<Sansho's "Original Silence">

Sky's Introduction

If you think there is something to lose, you are caught in the oldest trap. Unborn, where could you come from or go to? On any road, the dust of accomplishment will never cling to your feet. If there is the slightest doubt, see the following:

Main Subject

On his way to Incense Burner Mountain, Sansho decided to stop at Chang'an monastery to rest for the night. Seppo, the head abbot, seeing the monk coming along the road, met him at the front gate and asked: "Where have you come from"? Sansho, sensing a Dharma-battle, replied: "From the original silence". Seppo said: "In that case, now where will you go"? Sansho immediately said: "Where the golden carp can be out of the net". Seppo shook his head and commented: "Looking for a carp, you have found only the net".

Sky's Commentary

Suddenly, the brash monk's sandals became excessively loud with all his original silence.
A journey started in noise, ends in noise. Who could ever speak a clear word above such racket? When fishing, a careful approach is essential. Poor Sansho, mistaking the journey for the destination, attempted to weave a carp from the shadow a net.

Sky's Verse

No carp. No net.
Beyond coming or going -

Brushstrokes of sages continue to release the night.
A negative space of mountains.
Bright pools of fish.

Rinpoche's Teishō

At the gate,
A question was answered.
An answer was questioned.
Sansho, busy fishing in a dry stream-bed,
Missed Seppo's word of original silence.

Case 103

<Doumon Strikes the Evening Bell>

Sky's Introduction

When the mind is not in action, the evening bell will ring. How can you be sure? Even the cleverest will be misled in the dark of the day. What are the complications? See the following.

Main Subject

Several monks were talking in the courtyard when the head monk noticed it was getting dark and the evening bell had not been rung. Being curious, he went to investigate and found master Doumon sitting quietly by the temple bell. The head monk commented that it was almost the evening hour and the bell had not been rung – at which point, master Doumon leaped up and wildly struck the bell. The startled monk jumped back as the master slowly looked around, and then madly struck the bell two more times. Again, master Doumon carefully looked around, and seeing the flabbergasted look on the monk's face, calmly sat down, and said: "And after all that, still it is not evening".

Sky's Commentary

A shudder in the familiar twilight of earth.
Ascending to action brings only dragons in steam of white clouds.
Far below, Fools search at last light finding not a shard of history.

Acting but not looking.
Looking but not acting.

Sky's Verse

A pale specter of habitual light.
What is supposed to be is not what might be.

Evening or not,
In this looking and acting, all is betrayed.

Rinpoche's Teishō

Sound or no sound – the light was unchanged.
No evening.
No bell.

Case 104

<Nanto's "It is the Other">

Sky's Introduction

Somewhere a stone echoes-off a cane of black bamboo.
In an instant, all worlds are returned to the void.

Now. Before. After.
How can it be like that?
See the following.

Main Subject

After evening Banka, Engo said to Bokushu:
"They say it will be gone with the other*.
Can you give a turning word when form becomes void?"
Bokushu said: "Come back after now, and I will tell you".

Second Subject

Nanto came to the temple seeking Master Isan.
Isan's disciple Kozan said, "He is gone".
Nanto said: "With or without the other?"
Kozan replied: "Show me the other and I will tell you".
Nanto said: "It is the other".
Kozan replied: "Then why do you seeking Isan?".
Nanto could not answer and turned to leave –
Kozan called after him: "I will tell Isan you have gone with or without the other".

Sky's Commentary

Too complex to be accurate,
Too simple to be vague.

Words merge to wind without meaning.

When form becomes void,
With or without the other,
How can it be gone?

So admirable this – "Come back after now".
But it gives away too much of the remaining light.

Even though it was closer to gold than iron,
The two monks merely exchanged a circle of empty words.

While Nanto could not see through 'it',
Kozan, naming 'the other', also lost his only chance.

Sky's Verse

Not coming – Isan appears.
Not going, the other leaves the room.

Trying to split the moment,
Before and after cannot be found.

Rinpoche's Teishō

Stone and bamboo.
Infinite errors.
Perfect symmetry.

---

* From the Hekiganroku's Case 29 <Daizui's "It will be gone with the other">

Borrowed
<Lost Day>

In momentary architectures,
I saw your silhouette against a coming fusillade of storms,
As darkened gardens impossibly sang.

Over fallen fields of our fathers,
Evening bells took flight in a ringing of soft sparrow light,
As the departed stood with a glow of hands covering bowed heads.

It was only an ash of great music
Following you in scores of morning's alizarin tint -
Blood-spattered autumns and calm depressant of stars
Seeding our little time.

Entering autumn,
The evening inked a negative space of histories
In cold columns of black bamboo and white birds of falling snow.
It was a golden shroud of dusk
In spectral leaves around our feet -
Returning a lost day.

Crows in sumi-e shadows brushed a soot of calligraphy
In lamp-black and Ripasso against empty skies,
And bright hours ended in a wreckage of glittered zodiac
Where without warning -
Fields of frost lead the moldered voice of the cricket into winter.

In momentary architectures,
Under a ringing of soft sparrow light,
To awake was not possible
As all our borrowed hours began to replay –
And I saw your silhouette under empty skies,
As darkened gardens impossibly sang.

Cempasúchitl

After the velorio,
Clouds formed calaveras in wet straw of orange skies.

Hummingbirds circled an illusion of the spinning sun,
And a glare of streets carried the smoke of copal.

Perhaps forever, or for an evening,
Borders dissolved into preserved amber of long past hours,
Where distances could hold few separations.

As lanterns were lit,
A wake of voices and shuffled feet emptied the flickered zocalo,
Leaving only a child's paper marigold
As a gift and innocent question for the dead.

Churches are Empty

Churches are empty,
And evening came back to the cemetery
Like a lost dog.

Closing

I
Awakening to an empty house –
There was no year.

Closer to the end,
Autumn stopped in black and white gardens,
Where stone angels extended weathered hands.

II
Over twilight fields,
Premonitions of bells ascended from dark towers,
And a permanent lieder of crows
Spoke from vestments of trees.

Uncatalogued stars charted a long silence,
As carved doves looked out from the mausoleum
Where headstones in white bridges
Forged a passage to evening.

Without a defense,
Frost came in cold periapts for the living.
It was an empty house –
All our hours were closing
To autumn's monochrome garden,
As we extended weathered hands -

And there was no year.

Coming Night at Mathais Gardens

In pale largos,
Sparrows tuned a revised aria of failing light:
Grey eight's notes on *eau de nil* parchments of spring
Came in soaring promise of unfinished works.

Surrounding the Zocalo,
Empress trees painted forgotten histories
In a pale perse of cold fire.

Out of the aftermath,
We waited at the edge of pearl and glass-green oceans -
Voices of blue oat grass
Swaying in lunar blooms -
Where, with no response,
Ghosts continued to overrun autumn's yellow walls.

From the ending season,
Further apart -
It was a morning of our solemn human forms,
But the intended brightness had no purpose,
Channeling only threnodies from Zentralfriedhof to Père Lachaise.

In pale largos,
Sparrows tuned a failing light –
And Empress trees whispered some final color,
But ghosts continued,
And you would not have understood.

Cornfields and Graves

Where we walked,
A tired sun fell in gold-leaf and roses.
Dry cornfields knelt beside an ecru cut of dirt roads.

In a brittle wind,
Deserted woods surrounded a faint path,
Blocking some possible return.

Across snowy fields,
Shadows of nuns came back to dark rooms
Under cold rosary of stars.

Pale flowers of gravestones reflected the night
In winter's white caesura.

Beyond these tired suns –
I will come for you -
Long after the golden dust of exhausted summers have past -
Long after the noise of all our many-worlds has ended.

Corona – 1947
    <Astraea>

An arc of peregrinations too far from morning -
A brief glow over entangled landscapes,
Bringing all the shadows of the world.

The dead and the dying circled again in dry chants of mid-summer.

Years of fire and endless greys,
Arrived between the extremes of color and a long dark of passing stars.

In our waking –
It was only debris-fields of wind,
And old cottonwoods forming the death-rattle of an always-approaching dawn -

Eventually reddening.

Cuckoo at Deià
<For Robert Graves>

Old soliloquies in wood and ash
Composed a paused afternoon.
One bird continued.

From terraced fields,
Faint arias ascended La Serra de Tramuntana
In aural shades of Callet, Manto Negro and Syrah.

Over wild olives and a mosaic-clay of alizarin roofs,
A pale line between sea and sky emerged:
Transcribed Lapis Lazuli fused to Turquoise
In blue phrases of morning.

At Es Puia,
In viridity of all this growing light,
Rosemary winds painted still horizons
From ancient Lieders of the day.

In perfect remains of a lost spring,
One bird continued.

It was best to send friends away,
And remain alone in phrases of morning
With soliloquies of one bird
In turquoise, wood and ash
As if something could have been changed.

Darkness Across the West
    < fin de siècle>

Darkness across the West
Fermented a red field,
Where old cedars rustled in a faint storm of sparrows.

Across the river,
There was no ferryman,
As an autumn day came back
In the middle of Spring.

Unsure of identity,
A few ghosts walked a failed path along the dusk plaza -
Released from demands of a short life.

Without forgiveness,
It was the same evening,
Memory, like a stalker in the snow-lit streets,
Waiting for lost souls seeking passage,
Across all this darkness
Under old cedars and a faint storm of sparrows.

Death Poem

From what is called sleep –
Lightning delivered some momentary twilight,
Where there was no difference in brightness
Between an ending or a beginning.

Our time was long past
And would only stubbornly come again.

From what is called sleep –
In all this afterlight,
Who can say whether it is dusk or dawn?

Déjà vu III

Beginnings and endings reveal the Janus mask of now.

Autumn skies circled in dusk's static merge to dawn,
As crows inked a parchment of clouds
In familiar phrases of unfinished poems.

We had seen this before.

Now, only able to forget what will again be recalled,
It was a secret coming back at the end of beginnings -
A premonition not realized from hours of a single life.

It was a memory from our parallel days at the summer cottage,
But in the half-light,
We could never agreed on the order of events.

It was not about the sequence.

Now, under circling skies,
Perhaps not an anticipation of reddening leaves,
Nor remembrance of warmer days,
But merely something we had seen before
In fleeting impressions of a chosen reality,
As we waited under empty skies
For crows to piece together our unfinished poems.

It was dusk's static merge to dawn -
        The same endings and beginnings
        The troubled eternity of a single life,
        With a sense of our soon to be recalled histories -

Forming the Janus mask of now.

Desvelado

It is time to give up the illusion –
To give up the company of men,
And of having others to talk to
As winter sets in with its errant yellow sun.

It is time to give up memory –
To give up this persistent evening light,
Flooding every hour
In some lovely retelling of imaged histories.

You now see
That it is not for lack of company
That the solitary bird waits by these graves in icy cedar limbs,
Nor is it for lack of warmth that the fires burn out
From our oeuvre of unfinished days.

It is a myth of karma that can never to be corrected –
A wheel of dreams kept spinning by inertias of the dead.
It is stained blue fields of what might have been
Held in rosary windows of night.

It is time to give up the illusion,
Arcing over our wasted sleep
That is blanket and alarm -

A time to give up the beloved's memory
And the imagined fragrance of purpose
From all this lovely exhale of time -
As winter sets in with its errant yellow sun.

Dreamers

2:17 AM.

It was nothing like far thunder –
A pink noise of footsteps and wind,
But it was still snowing,
And we could not return to sleep.

Between the grey and the black,
We surfaced for some small eternity
Among old spaces of the dream and premonition,
Where I saw your face in light-years of all our ending words.
It was a moment.
It was no time.
Always.

Out of a short darkness,
City lights swarmed below us – vacant and losing color -
A recapitulation of faces from all lives
In the passing shock of memory.

It was a moment.
It was nothing like thunder,
Or the siren voices of snow.

It was a thin space between the grey and the black.
It was an old premonition of dreams,
Where it was snowing
And we could not return to sleep.

2:18 AM

Driving at Night

In a lento of dreams,
We drove past abandoned hulk of cathedrals.
You closed your eyes as the cars came too close.

There was a scent of boswellia, camphor and cassia.

Under stained-glass skies –
Chalices of light spilled through autumn larch,
And in the rear-view mirror,
The storm advanced in passacaglias of darkening birdsong.

It was a lento of dreams.
It was the scent of myrrh.
It was a recalled image that was yet to arrive.

On the windshield,
Stars swirled into rain,
And we drove into a country of night
Under collapsing waveform of falling leaves.

I would have stayed with you,
But there would have been no point.

Eikon

Stars became a wind of old light.

A pond of reflected iris
Bloomed a liseran purple of stained glass
Against the dream's closing eye.

Beyond sorrow,
I came to you in your sparse room,
Bringing a rough voice of ocean,
And glossolalia of extinguished candles.

Where we left them,
Far fields filled with aural flames of the mourning dove,
Seeded all this spring light.

In our remaining time,
There was still beauty,
As I held your bowed head in decaying arms.

Eikon II

Shadows climbed the stones of Moustiers Sainte Marie all night.

From this Autumn house,
Red blossoms spread around a recalled evening.

Elegies of children
Ran under copper leaves of ending skies,
Where the moon became a stone lantern in a snuffed candle of storms.

In this sad garden,
Out of desire and silence -
All our ghosts come back.

End of Days III

Everything rushed past even as nothing moved.

It was a still image:
A recalled evening with familiar faces -
Children running with cardboard skeletons,
And the light again slipping away.

Shadows came up blue gravel roads,
Mapping what had already been.

For a set of years,
The dead lived with us in this fragile house:
A bright loop of returning hours,
Coming back as if nothing had yet happened.

The sequence was never important.

It was the afternoon's perfectly failing light.
It was the exhale of final summers.
It was the book you put aside before sleep.

It was an exquisite moment,
Where everything was rushing past as nothing moved.

End of Evening

It cannot be stopped,
Even though there were barricades of autumn elms,
And an evening crowned with rich thorns of barbed-wire stars.

For you,
Torches continued to burn,
As gardens stretched into blackness of a bygone day.

Night's voices completed a partial requiem
Where stone angels ascended in weightless marble of carved clouds.

Years ago –
From the Cathédrale Notre-Dame de Reims,
We walked in a cold rain to the Cimetière du Nord –
The wineries were all closed,
And streets had more ravens than tourists.

Now here at the shore,
It cannot be stopped,
As the creation continues to overwhelm the creator.

Coming back, it was a barricade of autumn elms.
Everything had been completed and was about to begin again,
As I waited for clearing skies,
Recalling an evensong of wind
Like tides rushing through your tangled hair.

Enlightenment

Under receding tides of roseate light,
Snow over the courtyard
Whitened branches of a solitary olive.
No one could awake.

In the moment's held breath,
Asphyxiated skies closed in a sliver knot of stars around our pale forms.

Where we slept –
There were only Kyries of the white-wing dove,
As along the coast a slurred speech of ocean continued.

It was voices of mistral –
It was great distances collapsing to the darkness of our small room,
With receding tides of roseate light
Filling an olive tree with a bright seam of night.

There was snow over the courtyard.
It was only a short truce,
And no one could awake.

Enlightenment II

In our time of sleep,
There was a wind all night:
Anesthesiology of winter stars arced overhead
Keeping us apart.

Past waking,
Strange shapes roamed tarnscapes by the river.
It was only snow and a collection of ghosts at distressed windows.

Our summers collapsed from a dead spring's golden autumn day,
Out of time for what we might still do.

In our time of sleep,
There were roses of sunset by a silver fence,
And darkened hills were steep with burial cloth of gratitude and regret.

Past waking,
The fragment became the whole -
The moment - the eternity.

In our time of sleep,
Nothing will be explained,
As it was merely snow at distressed windows,
And an anesthesiology of winter stars
Keeping us apart.

Enso

Both alive and dead,
In a poker game of quantum suicide,
No cards were revealed -
Still, a cat sees though the superposition of its nine lives.

Where is the cat?

After some circling Sumi soot of dreams,
Too many dimensions became folded into Washi skies,
And morning collapsed into a gravity of spring
Where everyone walked out to all this perfectly calculated light.

After much deliberation,
The day was only a theory,
Where without permission,
Black holes waited in the cold outside the garden gate,
As festoon strings of stars counted a wild glow of rejected infinities.

There were no agendas.
There were no cats.
There were no marked cards -
There were only equations of songs,
And terrible spirals of unity balancing overhead in the dark.

So, with little left to do but heat water for tea,
A theory of twilight fields continued filling with snow,
Cataloged in the double slit of eyes -
Hopeful and unproven circles -
At once, alive and dead.

Entangled

Something happened here.

Past a childhood's red harvest,
Ice returned in white jasper and origami of winter trees.

It was a blood moon and cut-wrist of cathedral bells –
Daring all these vacant streets to matter.

Our shadows became embedded in markings of cold stones,
As snow whispered over a bright lament of red-shifted birds.

From a boat of preserved memory,
Fragile histories attempted to cross night's swollen river,
But it had been tried before.

Something happened here,
Where long beyond a single life,
In an ending red harvest -
Our entangled days were held together in shadows
And folded paper of winter trees,
Daring all these vacant streets to matter.

Evensong

Doves in 'call and response'
Composed a score of faint prayers.

Asleep before the end,
Bells of night flooded the ear's deaf canal.

It was your shadow by the garden gate:
No ash of angels –
No savior in a shirt of stars.

Under escaping heavens,
Nightingales sang in the clear light of Śūnyatā.

In 'call and response',
This same evening came back,
And we sat under skies of red leaves,
Where everything had never happened.

Exile

After light,
Your silence continued across vast spaces of the closing eye.

Shadows came over the threshold of our old house
Despite wild roses and ghost-white garlic's defense of slipping days.

A summer ends and comes back,
Only to end and come back.

Even one life is too many.

Face in Evening Clouds

For a moment,
It was some possible face in evening clouds.

All surrounding fields grew quiet,
And storms approached over long waves of amber grass.

Awaking at dusk,
There was no scent of burnt almonds –
No hyacinths in muscari choruses lighting a distant spring –
No purposeful dreams.
It was only an apnea of wind,
Piecing together arrhythmia of darkening skies far over our little time.

For a moment,
It was some possible face in evening clouds,
Approaching ghosts of imagined purpose,
And eidolons of remaining light
Far over our little time.

Fall

From this rough vision –
From this echoed space of afternoon –
I did not know where we would go.

You hovered over hushed landscapes:
Acrophobic parapets of ancient rock and air flutes:
White string of rivers painting vertigo horizons
In aerial velocities of the spinning sun.

In a flash of the long view,
Fallen climbers arced in slipping grips of passion -
A bone and dust of great distances,
Releasing orthoimages of the eye's final light.

From moments of the Fall –
Far below, crows drifted like dark gondolas
Along the axon's drained canal.

From this rough vision,
With a mounting cartography of accelerating shadows,
Wind in ending destinies filled a still point of the expelled breath.

In a flash of the long view,
It was an altitude of grace over a singular afternoon -
It was ending, and it was going to end.
There were last autumn colors approaching in lines of vertigo horizons -
Advancing details of landscapes getting clearer –
And I did not know where we would go.

Faux

Awaking to voices in morning's cold hall,
It was likely only whispers of wind,
Forming waves of ghosts walking up from the dark coast.

It was a purpose without history or patience -
Some silver speech that echoed across miles of receding coastline
We had left behind.

It was something out of our shared time –
It was a rustling light of cloned mornings,
And what possibly remained.

Awakening to voices,
Out of a long gust of memory,
It was only a mistranslation of what you had said,
In waves of our ghosts that had been left behind -

But it was not wind.

First and Only
<For Hildegard von Bingen>

As you leave,
The Eucharist is given in cold rooms of painted saints.

Choirs of blue fields were still with snow
 In a last winter,
Your book of a thousand years closes.

Blossoms of bells and Orion's cold flowers arced over your verdant sleep.

All night,
Cranes floated in shadows of dragons,
And a faint wind at the temple of the three hearts repeated your name.

From your vision-
In a clear voice – the world was created,
As your innocent dreams rose above antiphonal agonies of a absent God.

Forecast

Windows were closed against a coming storm.
There was a light over the garden that would not wait.

In a decayed autumn,
Small birds filled falling skies with twilight,
As the moon woke marionettes of shivered winter trees
In charcoal and bright obsidian.

Under a periodic table of stars,
With folded hands,
We ran through miles of falling leaves into unstable eternities.

In an anticipation of yesterday,
Under white murmurs of rain,
I saw you in the carved robes of a fountain.
It was of little concern.

Our season was over,
And closing windows against the storm,
We watched a light over the garden that would not wait.

Foreshadowing for a Desert Night

The spring night lights up with empty space of stars.

Awakening to an old chimera of the day
Is not what is difficult.

In the long fade –
We wandered about these canyons
Drunk with catastrophe,
As great phrases of finished light
Hovered at the end of an alley's white cupola.

Specters of Saguaro guarded the small hours.
Where we wrote our lives away,
Under golden blur of the Jerusalem thorn.

Fortune

In the moment before,
A light on your tongue
Extinguished a few strangled words.

You were running through dead wheat fields
In a glint of the still bronze summer.

Everything was closing -
The wind had stopped,
And the knife was cool and smooth in your tiny hand.

Garden of White Clouds
>"We continue, even if it's evening, even if it's fall".
>- Chiao Jan

On the way,
It was a pause of light –
A gap between dream and morning.

Long ago (*now*) –
A negative space veiled Incense burner mountain in a garden of white clouds.
Sand-raked oceans surrounded water-worn evenings,
Inking a senescence of youths forever into scrolled islands.

Like temples in mist,
Our poems were completed in absences as well as words.
It was the decay of a shakuhachi voice.
It was distant winds sensing stentorian silence,
With spoken sumi-e strokes from a last T'ang poet.

On the way,
It was a pause of light.

Old stone lanterns became lit with dusk -
But we continued,
Even though a path led nowhere –
Even though peach blossoms turned to glittered ice -
Even though dry leaves rustled in rouge-tinted hands of autumn stars.

Ghost Dance

Under returning Paha Sapa skies,
Tȟašúŋke Witkó wore a shirt of stars
Painted with the immunity of evening.

Across multiple worlds,
Current histories began to subside.

Once on Harney peak,
I saw all our years
Fall like a single leaf:
The child's chance of summer and revelation -
An exhausted dance of the sun,
Where all histories collapsed to one.

What is called the beginning and end
Entangle the same moment -
An intricate beadwork of time laid out like space:
Offering recurrent lives to correct eternal mistakes.

Under returning skies,
From the San Francisco Midwinter Fair Carnival,
Wovoka watched a first snowflake fall like a single leaf of years,
And with the immunity of evening,
Knew he had missed the point.

Ghost House II

It was going to snow.
Winter was now on the next little hill.

How it all grows dark
Here at the end of language.

Was it real?
At La Seu,
Cripples waited by dying votives long after dark,
Where tomorrow,
Morning fields would stretch into December beyond our agreement.

Once over our sad garden,
Lights in the sky held their great distances –
Where we could not sleep.
We were waiting at the end of language,
As our luminous details began to fade.

After the storm,
It was a clearing synesthesia of stars in the sound of diamonds and anise.
It was a requiem and non-repeating decimal of crows on the next
      little hill.

It could have been an Afillá rasp of wind
Forming Saetas over la Serra de Tramuntana.
It could have been a lament of those coming before or after,
Bringing soft nouns of enervated music and light.

Was it real?

Now, after youth,
Winter was on the next little hill.

It was going to snow -
And we almost noticed how it all grew dark –

Here at the end of compassion -
Here at the end of language.

Ghosts

From the long view –
Beyond details of the day,
Beyond a splitting of facts,
There is only the looking or the looking away.

Before the war,
Snow silenced a night's delayed choice.
After the war,
Snow silenced a night's delayed choice -
As if nothing could have been changed.

At the Chiesa di San Martino,
A few electric bulbs surrounded Mary in a dim nimbus of auric light,
And crowds gathered along the darkening harbor,
Where waiters in crisp sepia shirts set white tables
In a votive twilight's pale glare.

From the long view -
It was a few details of the day.
It was dusk's dawn of double-slit skies proving nothing.

Ghosts increase -
But there is only the looking or the looking away.

Glass Angels

For a last time,
Glass angels stared from the church transept:
A stain of twilight eyes,
Keeping watch over the winter streets.

Evening bells filled a quire of mountains in hollow voices,
As snow closed the courtyard with a still white requiem.

Not understood,
A glossolalia of articulate leaves
Surrounded the boulevard in ascended color.
It was a too-soon dark for those who could no longer stay -
Some aria of wind desaturating cold plane trees.

As we slept,
Circling stars rustled overhead
In a silver noise of altered histories.
An icy wind of poppies
Rattled in drugs of alizarin light,
Filling the plaza with dusk's open wound.

Arcades of December relinquished a passing memory.
Our stars were complete,
And everywhere in a stain of twilight eyes - not understood,
Cold white trees and glass angels
Kept watch over the winter streets,
For a last time.

Going Down

On marble floors of the closed cathedral,
It was only spilled blood from a sanctuary lamp
Where all the Vatican's books were of no help.

Hearing a Clock Somewhere Down the Hall

From the hotel balcony –
My notes said it was still evening.

At the threshold of winter,
Smoke from a cliché of votive candles darkened the duomo
In remembrance of smoldered ghosts.

Over tarnished hills,
Argent threads of falling water filled night's canvas
With Sumi-e brushstrokes of lampblack, comfrey, and ash.

Somewhere down the hall,
A clock scraped its aging feet along dry wood of old floors
Without a destination.

From the hotel balcony,
There was a false glow of something coming
As static years held us to the recorded day,
Where my notes said it was still evening.

Hegira

Frozen nights arrived beyond sound.
On the river,
A velocity of moonlight was incalculable.

Madmen walked ice-lit hills in heartbeat of steps -
A forbidden pattern of stars circling the bowed head.

Everywhere there was a recalled silence of the ending year:
Snow, soothing a troubled history to white.

By morning, there were no tracks -
Only cardinals in the clearing,
Bleeding a sunrise on linen fields.

I Have Seen you in the Darkening Garden

I have seen you in the darkening garden,
A shadow far from our empty house.
You stood in a rough effigy of the human form.

But it was too far from morning,
With a confetto of stars in cold distances
Blocking a return.

I have seen you in youth
On the unkempt streets of Rome,
Receding like a ghost
With scherzos of birds rehearsing
Over the cold statues of San Pietro.

It was only an anticipation of failing light,
It was only the return of old age –
With snow falling against a titian glow of kerosene windows all night.

I have seen you in the darkening garden,
Where you waited too far from morning –
With a slipping specter of purpose,
Blocking a return.

Icon

Seeking alms,
She looked up from shadow-worn steps of La Seu,
As a fallen rose becoming white winds of rushing wings.

There were no choirs –
And only a few children mocking what could not be understood,
As her face formed dark jewels of forgiveness
Against a fragile sun,
Under the wind of rushing wings.

Irrational Numbers

I saw us from where we stood.
Everything had already happened.

It was a ladder of sorrows.
It was all this distant space behind our eyes,
Tearing away remaining spirals of light

I saw us from where we stood,
Watching a sister in Pfarrkirche St. Mauritius
Brushing dust from a sunlit bench.

Here in a final image -
Pale storms came over the Pennine alps,
Making a single life seem real.

Spring continued,
Light was separating into all this void of space -
And our entangled worlds were failing.

It was a ladder of sorrows.
Everything had already happened,
As a sister brushed dust from a sunlit bench.

Isle of the Dead
<for Arnold Böcklin>

Alone in your repeated vision,
It was a progeny of evening storms, myth, and deliverance.
It was a copper-etch of multiple chances at a life -
Holding the moment in a small boat.

Here and for all to see,
With no Ferryman, there was only a short crossing
Stroked from white linens of last light.

Beyond grief,
Taking no unnecessary care –
The storm was always perfection.

Kyrie for the End of Spring

With no proof,
A faint music ended,
And darkening streets where we walked
Brought back voices of a bygone afternoon.

In resins of preserved light,
Robes of Tamarack trees anointed hands of your lost faith.

Awakening to a blue deafness of what remained,
Coming winter shadows circled open windows before morning
To no purpose.

There was someone and no one in the house.
There were darkening streets:
Failing eyes filled with incense of smoke and fire -
And with no proof, a faint music ended,
Where we were never gone and never here.

Lacrimosa

I

At first light,
It was a void of wasted hours and no time.

Some incidental music of Caspian terns
Came over the Wolfgangsee in waves of October:
Obbligatos for meaningless lives.

As the burial of the dead approached,
There was a sleet of cyclamen,
And falling flowers of snow over St. Sebastian's –
Everyone was long asleep.
It was wasted hours and no time.

II

In remains of this high village,
We came down under aeries of eagles,
Past old men waiting on benches by weathered chess boards -
It was a final sepia glow and images in vellum.

At the end of the old world,
Culture became a cul de sac of religion and trivia –
Everything was changing
And nothing was changed.

III

Blowing graupels of winter's pointillism
Finished a pentimento of faces over the Altstadt,
Where choirs along the Mozartplatz sang lacrimosas against the cold.
It was Christmas and no one noticed how everything was returning.

At first light,
Morning became quiet with an emptiness that comes of vindication.
Everyone was long asleep,
As snow continued over St. Sebastian's
In a void of wasted hours and no time,
But It was Christmas, and no one noticed.

Late October

Evening's purple ecstasy fades.
The lonely fields.

In white blossoms of headstones,
A winepress of stars
Crushed a childhood's fragrant memory.
It was a long erosion of color,
And telophase of ghosts.

Past October,
An encaustic glow of angels arrived at last light.
Unkempt fields became ever-wilder,
As Beech and Hornbeams swirled in preserved amber,
And frost translated the stopped day.

In a lilac freeze of morning,
Autumn was suddenly over.

At last, transient -
I swept the porch
and heated water for tea.

Listening to a Crow at Lake Biwa
<For a Minor Kyoto Poet>

Under unfinished stanzas of a single crow –
Shadows in cypresses' feldgrau
Moved in clock hands beyond the twilight of your open door.

In the village of your birth,
Figures in darkening dirt streets
Walked in rhythms of harvest scythes
Where nothing was completed.

From these rough drafts of recursive lines,
Never staying in one place,
Revisions of the moment were not possible.

In the dark – ghosts waited for the returning charade of morning,
And cypresses danced by the lake outside of time,
As you set aside your work –
As you waited for nascent futures,
Listening to the distant catastrophe of a single crow.

Long Count

The long count ends.

It grows dark again,
Where all these created worlds continue in the exhale of minor lives.

The witnesses are mostly asleep,
And snow ends the day in a scent of aging lilacs and unkempt gardens.

From colder blossoms of some missing time,
Shadows like ravens waited in a Deja vu light -
Never allowed to forget.

Where you stood –
All of what is called time past will never be closed,
As evening's oxytocin exhausted a history of the never-passing moment.

Calendars continued in circles.
Unmasked Kachinas came to dance on the village square,
As time restarted again beyond your will.

Without the blessing of anyone,
Simulations will end
As choirs continue in echoes of Palestrina's *Nigra sum sed formosa*
Long after saint-shrouded cathedrals have converted to ash.

The long count ends.
It grows dark again.
A few lives will matter.
Creations cannot not be absolved.
No one will be forgiven.

Los Endos

I believed I was awake to old age outside a Tuscan village
In a house of stone and lavender.

There was no date,
And from the perpetual storm
Over advancing afternoons,
Clouds blew across curtains of dancing fields.

I believed I was awake.
It was a house of stone and lavender.
I put on a thin white shirt -
And wrote until the end of morning.

Lost Image

Fountains of poplars spilled an ash of gold
From Montefiorelle to Castello D' Albola.

Even with no wind,
Your hand trembled like a geranium in autumn's pale fire.

Lure

In these clouds –
Only luminous remains of angels and evening.

By the buildings of government,
Rivers came back in ancient sonatas.
Crows watched from céladon flames of cypresses
Becoming a ashen wind.

Night and damp rust of stars,
Knelt over you in a blue fire that could not be contained.

A senescence of asters and goldenrods
Rippled in a pool of drowned hours,
Waiting for some remnant of distressed light
That was never going to arrive.

From a empty church,
Finished rosary shadows fell in shards of color
Where altar-candles painted a raiment of tortured silhouettes.

In these clouds – a few luminous remains.

None of this will be recalled.

Magdalene

At evening,
A ruin of bells and your silence cannot be suppressed.

Clouds like sparrows came in grey linens of lament
Over dying waves of golden ferns.

A stone wall held a wind of empty streets.
In the dark –
Black ash of poppies stiffened in violet snow.

Far from the fires of men -
Where you walked,
Plainsong notation of dead stars darkened an old forest path.

At the end of autumn,
The moon rose as a worn nimbus over white villages in a completed
　　　red sleep,
And garnet twilights continued in cold shards
Of our long-disputed memory.

Without judgment,
It was a ruin of bells –
A life leading nowhere –
And worn robes of night sheltering your silence along these empty streets.

In a clear song of sparrows,
It was a still field of golden ferns,
And plainsong of dead stars,
Calming your miscarriage of angels.

Mallorca - Autumn

September alarms faintly began.

A cold light of Spain gathered in grey bell towers:
A pause of islands
Beyond illusions that there was some recorded past.

At La Seu,
Decayed colors of stained glass
Descended in transcriptions of fire:
Old wood of empty pews embalmed in magenta and gold.

Out in la Serra de Tramuntana,
It was only the failing light over Alaro
With Nacreous clouds troubling a night of sleep.

From a morning that would not come,
Agoraphobic fields were littered with rocks, sheep, and fog.
It was archival hours beginning a long count
Outside our small night room.

At open windows –
Cold Almond trees whispered in white winds.
It was pentimentos of the past -
And I could almost hear a pause of islands
Amid faint alarms of September.

Mary in the Night Room

There is a night room –
Stillness and blue voices of falling water -
A garden outside a reflex of dreams.

Red forests awakened before morning
And grackles became gargoyles
Along darkened rooftops.

There is a night room,
Where oceans speak
In whispered resignation of lost lives –
Wave after wave of silvered talismans protecting nothing.

Out in locked memorial grounds,
Stone angels crouched in alcoves,
Waiting for the return of all our small hours.

From a first winter night,
There were no lights at the shuttered church -
Colors began to fail:
Like Pythagoras approaching the underworld –
Like Mary waiting in the night room -
Like a stillness of suffocated speech,
Where we drown in a red forest of submerged stars.

Everything was moving further apart -
There was light coming along the rooftops,
But it was not morning -
It was a reflex of surrendered dreams –
It was a premonition of too many worlds,
And chimera that we had more time left.

There is a night room –
A garden outside a reflex of dreams -
Lost lives waiting for morning,
And the return of all our small hours.

Masque

Over our solemn forms,
Cold calligraphy of crows
Darkened an evening of silhouettes.

We have built of wind,
A Greek labyrinth of never-passing time.

We have built of water,
A talisman of whirling poems
Washing ashore in drowned speech of what was to come.

We have built of fire,
A house of night –
Where foreign constellations declined above black fields
Before and after our exhausted hours.

From a masque of precognition –
Stars bloomed in an overgrowth of thorns,
Lighting ashen prayers for morning.

It was only a calligraphy of crows
In a never-summer where years slipped away
Far short of prayers for morning,
Leaving the silhouettes of our solemn forms.

Mendocino 1979

Along the coast,
Residual voices of the day came back in waves,
Like footsteps down the hall.

It was a ringing in our ears of autumn light -
A tinnitus of some simple sleep,
Where we had used up all our time.

It was watered sunsets over scripted oceans,
As daily, everyone came out to watch –
A mix of sun and water -
At the motionless speed of light.

We waited under repeated pigments of dusk -
A meeting of strangers, tides and pentimento of memory.
It was cremation fires –
Time fossilizing the bones of our hands into amethyst and shared carbon.

In the grey sparrow light,
If we closed our eyes,
All worlds would have collapsed.

Perhaps it was only phrases of wind
In evening's artificial color -
Painting a pink-noise of words against black cliffs.
Perhaps it was only the settling of this old house.

In repetitions of tired anger or repentance -
It was a premonition of where we might have been:
Hearing only waves of footsteps down the hall,

It was a ringing in our ears -
Residual voices of the day,
Where we had used up all our time.

Metaphysical

Woodsmoke and lines of ocean
Surrounded your waking in selenium and sea holly.
Arbutus groves approached in colors of a blooming bister sun.

From this cottage of wild capers and rain,
It was a brief violence of poems,
Woven in hazel waves of fountain-grass,
At the end of revisions.

Never at ease –
Alone on ivory cliffs,
A glacial silt of storms anointed your face in aged linen and sage.

When the moon had risen high in the sky –
Clouds traced back-lit pennons of prayer flags
Rippling over these silent islands in elements of color,
And at the end of revisions,
I came back to the shore in a brief violence,
Slowly combing seaweed and damp clematis from your tangled hair.

Meteor Fall over the San Juan Mountains

With no sequence to our winter,
Silence and light conceived a polyphony of acapella stars.

After the fall,
Night and luminous ice traced the ridges of our hands
In a palmistry of hidden maps.

Ending seasons of what may be recalled
Arced over the shadows of men.

It was all choice and no free will.

In timelines of fire -
With no sequence to our winter,
A meteor in some bright veil of angels filled the gathered evening:
Burning out forever -
Architectures of the dream's false awakening,
And echoes of our lost promise.

It was a chance of choice,
And no free will.

Ministry

Dark kerosene of streets mapped a flickered history.

At the Duomo,
Lunar choirs offered an incense of empty praise.

Pale ghosts momentarily formed in frost at rosary windows,
And glittered candles of ice lamped a nominal procession
For a burial of the dead.

After the mass,
Residual shadows grieved by silver votives
That shook like a seizure of cold stars.

A small grey bird sang in the churchyard,
As a spiral glow of exhausted worlds
Encircled our brows in fingers of dried laurel and a long-passed light.

Leaving you behind was not a choice.

Mnemonic

Red incense of Buddhist monks
Cannot hold back a silk of evening.

Beyond a shadow of philosophies,
Without instruction -
Silence returns across a long bridge of stars

Long ago, yesterday -
Rikyu walked away from the garden path
Into magenta maps of morning -

Trusting only to an entangled glow of the lark's implied song.

Moon and Star Over Île de la Cité

Spring continues.
Crickets anesthetize the blue evening.
A scimitar of moon ferments a yellow field,
As runes of cedars rustle to a faint storm of sparrows.

Along the Rue Massillon,
Ghosts walked a failed path -
Held in expectations of a recalled life.
From a path of night and smoke,
There was nothing to recover.

A spire fell in ash and orange light.
The evening star remained as bright and distant as ever.

Without forgiveness,
Spring continued as our same hours came back
Where everything began and ended once again.

Morning at St. Magdalena

One hundred years
And light keeps soaking back through ice and lavender of your garden.
Battlements of poppies forged pennons with no allegiance.
Chisel-cut crosses softened in silver blades of iris-light.

Over these thrusting islands,
Fields angled away in slow parabolas.
The summer became still in green wheat and empty skies.

In this original brightness,
A silk-frost of morning sanded old mountains to rough prayers
And stone-washed rosaries
Where a wildfire of heavens burned away chants of the mourning dove.

Like water over rock,
Or storms in dawn's blue reed -
At first light:
One hundred years -
A tapestry of gardens,
And the myrrh of your lost voice.

New York Evening – Autumn 1984

Sparse crowds shadowed wet streets,
In an asphyxiation of color.
There was a scent of anise and eucalyptus.
Crows were full of trees.

It was a distant hiss of mistral.
It was a death-rattle of dishes from the Felix,
And blue and white flowers like stars
Littered the corner of West Broadway and Grand.

Rain whispered a cadence and cascade
In theia mania for no one.

Along the city's stone canyon,
Our silhouettes became Motherwell umbras
Staining a senescence of nights we had left years before.

In red pennons,
A few remaining maples
Defended against October's last siege
All the way to the East village.

At West Broadway and Grand,
It was an asphyxiation of color,
And crows were full of trees.

Nightscape

At 20 degrees,
Listening to Hildegard von Bingen plainchants,
History became suspect,
As if we were never here.

We were never here.

Nineteen Pictures from an Exhibition

I
<Winter Light>

At the end of anticipation,
A wind of birds brushed a canvas in dark remains of summer -
It was a gold of evening completing old maps of our folded hands.

Over a series of repeated nights,
Voices in the dream's motet bled Kyries of dead stars.

Across the piazza,
Couples became a union of ash and shadow,
As silver thorns of heavens circled in black ice.

At the end,
It was all these multiple worlds that covered our faint memories of sleep -
Dark pennons of summer,
Completing golden maps of our folded hands.

II
<Manfred at Moenchblick>

The light was immense,
But our images were becoming too faint to recall.

In a fever of night,
Lessons of humility followed in dreams,
Without our consent.

Before morning,
We circled in a catalepsy of imagined choice,

Under silhouettes of Chough wings
Forming brush-strokes in lamp-black and ash.

The light was immense, But we could not catch up.
And our images were falling further behind.

III
<Ponts Couverts>

Across Petite France,
Eight-notes of ambulances
Delivered watercolor voices of rain and red lights.

Events unfolded under broken glass of storms -
Everything had been said,
But nothing was final,
And old lights glittered in a wreck of history along the canals.

IV
<At the Line>

Waking after waking –

We saw unfamiliar patterns of stars.
Dreams emerged from ink of black skies,
And Sumi-e stroke of faces outside of time.

It a was momentary eternity – Crows circling all night,
Bringing a silence of our collapsing hours.

I saw you at the end of blue days -
A graceful wraith of old age.

You had marigolds in your hair the shade of autumn larch.

Waking after waking,
We were coming back to the beginning.
Crows circled in a twilight country,
Back when skies promised rain – dreams emerged,
And you had marigolds in your hair.

V

<Bannockburn>

Sirens sang –
It was plainchants of lost sailors in sketches of verdigris tides,
And drowned voice of calendars, out of time.

You stood at the helm:
A doppelganger in unique shadows,
Portending a silence at the end of the year.

Without a compass,
Overhead, stars wrecked in a dead reckoning of completed light.
There would be no time for last words.

The seas were still,
But avoiding an artistry of rocks
Was never possible -

Sirens sang –
Airless dreams advanced in our mirrored silhouettes.
The coral light was perfect,
But silence approached,
And there would be no time for last words -

Ghost ship or not.

VI
<Cepheus>

Along 49 steps,
The sequence ended:
A cul-du-sac of cold fire and incomplete maps.

Crossing the path,
Stars swung like censers over long distances.

We found markers in abandoned gardens,
Where old wood of fruit trees
Scraped skeletal branches in a black chorus of wind.

At the end of myths –
Marble urns littered the evening
In imprints of the human form.

Along 49 steps,
We had been walking in circles,
Born of incomplete maps.
The winter was now upon us,
And we knew that the light had never been real.

VII
<Dates in Stone>

A passing cloud darkened an afternoon.
It was not on any calendar.
Softly, rain chiseled dates into smooth stones.

Across the west,
A galaxy of crows moved away too quickly to count.

From infinite variations of the moment -
Everything ended and began,
As we stepped back in shadow –
Where rain softly chiseled dates into our darkened stones.

VIII
<Colors for a Dead Poet>

Footsteps in a storm
Wore away rough cobbled streets.
Nights already seen.
Kerosene lantern of stars,
Flickered to a stained-glass fall.

IX
<In a Water Garden>

Creeping Jenny, Taro, and cardinal flowers
Surrounded a sutra of fountains.

Hearing requiems of rain,
We waited beyond achievement.
The gardens were calm,
As a storm light blossomed
In the receding glow of empty hands

X
<Light Going Out>

Dusk crossed the border from Mexico –
An immigration of shadows and a tired sun.

It was a secret the authorities already understood.

At the San Jacinto plaza,
An ancient music ended.
Without documentation,
Clouds continued passed all checkpoints well past evening

It was light going out.
It was amber marigolds for the dead.
It was relics of art in ash from what was left of our time.

It was only the intention to stand for something.
It was a secret the authorities already understood.

XI
<Los Alamos>

Over black robes of the Jemez mountains,
A cold wind fanned coals of orange lights.

Mutations of cottonwoods and silver poplars,
Extended dark arms under an experimental vaccine of stars.

Our fires had always been receding,
But now looking west - it was clear.

XII
<Figures on a Beach>

At the edge of winter,
In pale pointillism on distant headlands,
Grazing herds waiting under Prussian skies.

From a lunar wash of golden chain trees,
It was a superposition of youth and old age,
Bringing back a futurepast when the night was unclaimed,
And the world was still young.

XIII
<No Translation>

Desire breeds a birth of ghosts.
Clouds like phantoms
Came at nightfall in a palladium green of the slipping spring.
From here, shadows only grew colder within this aging house.

It might have been a scratch of voices,
Or failing clockwork of ghosts coming to the locked door -
As a night of vacant skies swirled in some bright drain of finished light.

Soliloquies of wind continued. To awake was never possible.

En todos los mundos posibles, no hay nadie.

XIV
<Exile>

As they groomed our long sleep,
And I will tell you what I know:
There was no sequence –
As my hair was grey and brown and black.

Always, we slept under a blanket of static hours –
A Sargasso Sea of circling dreams -
Recursive nights piecing together mosaics of memories,
Not our own.

We saw clear images of flickering light,
But the small details were always out of place.

I will tell you what I know:
Humans tire of life in this rich poverty of creation,
Where none of the cuts in the world could heal.

Again, by night –
We awoke to an open window of cold violets and snow.
It was a development of character and practice for a long journeys.

I will tell you what I know –
There was an unremembered scar on my hand.
It was a sequence without chapters, where my hair was at once -
Grey, brown, and black -
The details were out of place,
And the world could never heal.

XV
<Prayer for the Departed>

What will it mean when yellow leaves erase your face?
What will it change when we fall into blue waves of the draining day?

In a dance and ecstasy of the autumn soul,
Red choirs of elms emerged,
And days circled a steady compass of the spinning sun.

In dust of your streets, we became soaked with stars -
Finally, letting go our ancestors,
Beyond what had passed or what would come.

Under a glittered boat of rustling elms,
Days circled a steady compass of the spinning sun -

It was a yellow dust of your streets,
And blue waves of the draining day -
In a dance and ecstasy of the autumn soul.

XVI
<Satori>

From premonitions
Of nothing past the moment -
Fire of leaves increased.

XVII
<Storm of Roses>

Not contained,
The light passed by.

We lost speed coming through a dense glow of dreams:
It was a storm of roses.
You stood in our young garden,
By a steep path bordered in colors I had seen before.

A night of too many lives sketched a darkened sky.
Something came up from the Southwest -
In what seemed like a choice,
But it was merely carbon shadows of all that had already happened.
There were wet fields leading a return to evening,
As doves called down a pink noise of encaustic light.

The light passed by –
It was an exhale of what we had been given:
Lives that seemed like a choice,
Where you waited in a night of too many lives,
Bringing a storm of roses.

XVIII
<Styx>

At Feneos,
Dusk sketched a negative space over mount Cyllene.
It was only a grey field of winter trees.

In chants of ghosted leaves -
Everywhere charades of lost color drained into documented days.

From a fifth circle of morning
Without incident,
Shadows waited by the river for passage.

We were too tired to begin again.

No history.
No crossing.
No ferryman -
And only a grey field of winter trees.

XIX
<Ferns Return>

Spring clouds of white ice.
Winter gardens in still sleep.
One jade scroll breaks through.

Nocturne

Winter's cauterized light
Closed white wounds of Corpus Christi in fire of frost.
We were only here for a short time.

A small mass of the lark completed two thousand years of stillness.

Behind us,
A wind of footsteps came along the wooden stairs of October,
Where amber fields ended in a harvest of our few words.

Coming back like a funeral cortege,
The evening released black mastiffs of night -
Where our shadows became stridendos of skeletal December trees.

A conclave of crows circled overhead in a *fumata nera* of decline.
We were only here for a short time.

In winter light,
A small mass of the lark continued,
And shrouds of clouds covered a flight of the exile,
As in stillness, we waited on the wooden stairs of October,
And put out our hand to the black mastiffs of night.

Oracle
<Die Geheimnisse>

From night's purple canon,
Storm's bloomed above an abyss of fall's sacrarium.

Unceasing,
Counted bells swept over black locust trees
In ticking glacial voices.

Behind the eye's closing firmament,
Crumbled gardens could only follow.

At old windows,
A glittered nimbus of stars calmed your smooth brow,
Where in an empty room –
So quiet, a blue decay of hyacinth graced what was left of our time.

Before frost-carved rosaries,
The savior's face seemed to appear -
But it was faded poppies in noscapine, rosewood, and cinnabar,
Delivering evening's dark opiate.

Beyond the locked village gate,
A final gold of still fields
Released the soul's fire in rich afterglow of autumn fruit.

Past twilight,
Voices of the dead washed this swaying island of sea-oats and stone
      botonées,
As wicks of cypresses flamed up with insane light.

On the threshold of meaning,
Sacred music fell from injured hands.

Over a cold sleep of ivory wheat,
Choirs of crows tangled above our bent heads,
In all the we have desired and neglected.

By the river, lanterns were being lit,
And crumbled gardens could only follow.

Forgotten again,
All this shall be set aside.

Oubliette

Reading our words,
We have come to where we could not come.

In the emptiness of the old villa,
The dusk lake hung like a simulation at open windows -
Blue infinities past sleep,
In a clone of autumn beyond our reach.

We are our oubliette -
Waking in the small hours to matins of turning fields,
As meaning escaped like charcoal birds
Into paper heavens.

Above the duomo,
Stars swung in unapproachable thuribles:
A hiss of finished light
Above the haggard faces of painted saints.

From all this distance,
It was our lives that could not be recalled -
A redacted detail of years
Where accomplishments were staged,
And morning never came.

Reading our words,
We have come to where we could not come.

It was the end of evening,
Or merely wind's mass in antiphons staging another night –
A cul-de-sac of static time without freedom.

It is said that something like angels watch over the living,
But they are not angels,
And we are not the living.

Out of Alfacar

My hands touched holy water at a singing cistern of morning.

There was a ringing in my ears of passing light.
There was a table of white Spanish roses
Falling into some last days of August.

With rain and grey songs of a few doves -
Bringing only a book of your poems,
We walked the Nacimiento De Fuente Grande
Without any discernible history.

It was not a pardon,
As shadows filled all these decaying gardens
Under Icons of lost heavens.

It was a singing fountain and roses of morning
Mapping your great silence -
A murmur of doves under the shade of alder and almond trees –
Or just the ringing in my ears of passing light.

Pentimento
    <silhouette>

I

In this entangled light –
Morning was already here.
Fires on the mountain had burned out like our aging house,
And the harvested grape had faded to a cold mauve fire.
There was nothing left but to let the moment pass.

Across all our many worlds,
Evening's controlled bleeding could not be stopped.
It was a half-light of waking.
In this found light,
Clouds seized-up to vast comas,
Where we could not shake off the dream.

The time of brightness was over.
A persistence of memory
Crumbled into a gold cloth of empty hands,
And the streets were submerged under red leaves and night,
As we willfully forgot our collection of small days.

The fires had burned out.
Morning was already here.

II

In dreams it was all given away.

From remaining scratches of light,
We sat on the terrace
With a cacophony of martins under violet Rothko skies,
As children played with paper ghosts
Against the approaching storm.

Under a complex logic of decline,
The streets were drowned in a failing eyesight of red leaves,
Where in this entangled light,
It was all given away in dreams, -
Knowing the morning was already here,
With nothing left to do but let the moment pass.

Plight and Premonition

Spotted Towhees sang in blue needles of a Montgomery spruce.
It was still light.

Outside,
Cold ghosts spiraled out of the attic of autumn.

Preserving the embalmed day,
A few chrysanthemums bled a last fallen color.
The upper fields were closed for the season,
As spires of stars became distant votives of exhausted light.

Regardless of what year most people supposed it was,
Worn calendars continued to slip through fingers of the living.

It was still light.

At your grave,
I knew nothing would change,
And that I would – against my will,
See you again.

Prayer After the Canon

By the cathedral,
Orion ascended over roses and barbed wire.

Magnificats echoed into a cruet of lead-crystal nights,
Where heat of heavens encircled your throat
In amulets of suspended fire.

After a red harvest,
My hands became cut with stained glass of receding light -
And – in a prayer after the canon,
I walked these darkening streets
Like the last man.

Predator

Autumn coins of aspen leaves anointed eyes of the dead.

In funeral isles of arroyos -
An unprotected perimeter of night continued.

Long after summer,
Piñon crosses emerged in infrared prints of night and snow.

From a shadow of Jaguars, some brief pain
Carried you in a boat of the canyon's past tense heaven toward morning.

Looking for safety,
With no ability to awake -
In Jicarilla songs of light,
Here - at the end of the world -
Here - remembered or not,
There were coins of leaves covering sleeping eyes -
Where we all awoke to torn light of the new day.

Premonition

Vapor drawings of birds in their bodies of winter
Ended a desolate day in rosaries of pale color.

Spring will come up from twelve stations of Notre-Dame of
        Moustiers-Ste-Marie
In yellow broom and bells of morning.

Fog will anoint the valley in sun-shafts of Paschal candles,
And white robes of small altar boys.

Beyond oleanders of youth and thurible-smoke of circling seasons –
We came with empty hands,
Receiving a communion of remaining light,
For all we could not have been.

Quincunx
    <Nostalghia>

After what you once believed,
Farolitos in the still garden counted winter's blue steps.

Stellar Jays ascended in slow afterlight of cathedral bells,
And feet-worn stones of the plaza.

Over the Sangre de Cristo's broken arch,
Faint ghosts of snow climbed to constellations of crosses and silver wood.

In a growing espalier of shadows,
Smoke of piñon fires delivered a suspended afternoon.

At distressed glass at the Basilica of St Frances of Assisi,
Fingered rosaries of frost numbered a knotted circle of hours,
Where after what you once believed -
Votives glittered in the dark,
Counting winter's blue steps.

Realization

Pale wind of lavender doves
Floated to flowers over the cours saleya.

You were the figure on the fountain -
Shadowed eyes behind falling water and red leaves,
An event horizon I could never escape.

In the morning,
It was a numb glow of floral light across your face,
Where I knew you had given up on this world.

Reconsidered on Night Streets Around Piazza Navona

Night wrapped around these cobbled streets
In luminous mushrooms of Italian stone pines.
Red forgeries of the war still remained.

Stars formed faint notes on parchment skies
In acapella voices from San Pietro to Giardino delle Cascate.

A shadowed speech of fountains whispered how close the end is to
    the beginning.

With no escort to morning –
Coming back to the hotel past Sant' Eugenio,
Later - I read your poems far into the night,
As fountains whispered,
And night wrapped around these cobbled streets.

Perhaps we both have been wrong.

Red Wing Blackbirds at Jalama Beach

Winter afternoons continued
Over stress of ancient grapevines and white winds of ocean.

Along the coast,
Feathered clouds formed lines of aerial waves -
Voicing the day's preserved light.

Red wing blackbirds sang in shadows of a thorn tree,
As twilight returned in clear determination and forgiveness.

In the song is the salvation.

Revelation

At the end it was quiet -
Inchoate ghosts huddled together,
Repeating worn sentences from all lives.

But it was the calm of Samurais who do not care if they live or die.

Setting a Clock

10:37 p.m.

Out of some small eternity between dusk and dawn -
The light traced a sequence too brief to follow.

Then all the clocks caught up with us.

Unnoticed,
There were familiar shadows in the corner of an autumn room.
Purpose waited like Orpheus approaching the underworld.

We objected to a plagiary of dreams,
But the windows were locked,
And wounded red stars came over the Olympics like zombies,
Futilely trying to break into this dark house.

It was a small eternity too brief to follow,
Then all the clocks caught up with us.

10:38 p.m.

Shadows at the Harbor

Pink noise of distant voices,
And folded nets of the day.

Shadows lined a pier of evening
With wreckage of multiple histories.
The sun was a smudge of rain, wind, and salt.

Your voice became blue shards
Breaking on terrible reefs of what we had not said.

Sage storms stacked stones for drowned sailors –
Scrawling lost names in tossing pearl and seaglass of waves.

Waiting to exhale,
We could only fall into cold arms of the moment.

Across the bay,
From approaching rhythmic lines,
There were footsteps of deaf oceans -
There were final noises in colors of intent -
A wreckage of history -
Your distant voice,
And folded nets of the day.

Simulation

Histories began to fall away,
As gaps in the world appeared.

Faces in the mirror
Were not the children of men.

Waking at night,
The house was quiet,
And stars arced over the time we had left
In beautiful silver thorns.

It was repeated voices of wind -
It was aneurysms in the violated hour of dreams -
There was nothing to do.

Histories began to fall away.
The house was quiet,
And in the mirror,
We were not the children of men.

Small Bridges

By El arco de la Drassana,
I passed my shadow
As if there was no problem.

Around this island town,
Cataloged stars came over a tsunami of black hills to the north -
It was a child's drawing on manila paper –
A scrawled day in charcoals darkening the coast.

At the Basilica de Santa Maria,
Afterlives of color rained from Catherine windows
Over careful rows of empty wooden chairs.

In a tincture of cathedral dusk,
Promised years of silence advanced.
There were a few small bridges left to night.
No one spoke.
It was ending,
And it was going to end.

In codas of confused light,
Spring disappeared into cold hills above Deià
In white dust of abdicating almond trees,
Littering la Serra de Tramuntana with a snow of pale ghosts.

At the end of simulations,
It was afterlives of color -
And I recalled passing my shadow,
As if there was no problem.

Snow Garden

At dawn,
With no one coming,
We awoke to syzygy of ice blossoms
And whispered rumor of spring leaves.

Over this cold house,
White frocks of a late snow
Blanketed troubled landscapes.
From morning's pale remains,
Dreams dissolved into cartographs of undiscovered light.

It was a few ghosts at steamed windows.
It was the wind's acapella score in voices from our past.

A few birds sang over mandalas of frost,
And a paroxysm of what is called 'now'.

At dawn –
Calculating the end,
There was no one coming to bridge the gap and chaos of distant stars,
And we awoke to blossoms of ice,
Where we could only begin again.

Snow in the Desert

From 68th Avenue north,
Snow suspended a redacted afternoon.

Everything was stopping –
Voices became distant,
And glowing streets looked like luge runs
In primary pennons of vacant color.

The occasional privacy winter affords has no price.

Sound Without Fury

The hour stood still.

In the dusky cathedral,
A small group practiced Handel's concerto for lute and harp.

Ghosts came up from the rain-draped streets of Petite-France
In a ceremony of shadows.

Beside the canals,
Xanthous voices of poplars grew cold,
As stars turned to ice over the next little hill.
The hour stood still.

We could not make a difference.

Spiegel im Spiegel

From this aging house,
Days were Starlings passing in graffiti at silvered windows.
On winter's hardening lake,
Fractals of ice mapped recursive afternoons.

Those who had lived here before,
Appeared again at late autumn -
Watching from October gardens
In the sad gazes of sculptures.
In the failing light,
They kept some great distance,
As the hours continue to replay.

From this aging house,
Our shadows also lingered in stone, wax and reflected fire -
Mirroring the hands of candle-cleaners at Saint-Étienne-du-Mont.

Watching or watched,
We are movements in a long set of mirrors,
And only those we imagine we see.

From this aging house,
Watching from October gardens:
The Janus face of the stalker and the stalked.

Storm

At the end,
There is all the time in the world.

She said a storm was coming.
It was already here.

Rain etched dead faces on tarnished silver windows,
And waves out on Le Sirenuse archipelago scripted revised lines -
Sentences from untranslated images of everything that had passed.

She said it would only be a moment.
It was long before and far after.

We came ashore
As if there were no dreams –
As if we were here –
Like ravens out of a bell tower
Revising a dusk wind
Over gold of dirt streets.

She said we were expected.
We were not.

Light years became exhausted in the dark,
Everyone was too far from shore to find a way back.
Most were being left behind.
It was understandable.

It was a storm of white-caps of our best lines –
Words of drowned poets –
A mirage of days –
And ending chaos of poems.

She said a storm was coming,
As the day slipped through our fingers
And familiar rain etched our long-dead faces
On tarnish silver windows –

With all the time in the world.

Sunset Tint
<Twelve Hours of Hokkus >

I
Pale lilac blossoms –
Silver sails on ocean sky:
Blooming waves at dusk.

II
Winter cloaked Saguaro
In surprised cold white cassocks:
Shadowed silent priests.

III
The body won't last.
Dusk fills autumn wheat with light,
And first ghosts of snow.

IV
From this bright valley,
With shadows of our old age –
Petals of clouds came.

V
Pixels of faint snow
Held failing light of evening: Mountains bridged to clouds.

VI
Scrawled on dusk's parchment
White stars of autumn iris:
Spent constellations.

VII
The unreal moment.
A Planck-length of evening ghosts:
Timeless illusions.

VIII
For some counted hours,
In the grey light, she swept snow
From the graveyard path.

IX
Silver shoji screens
Show silent soliloquies:
Secret silhouettes.

X
A coterie of crows
Are brushstrokes on twilight skies:
Amanuensis.

XI
In a paused dusk wind
White birds bloomed to bright flowers:
Lost blossoms of spring.

XII
An evening of wind.
White prayer flags at the summit:
Pale chrysanthemums.

Swans at Vitznau

Above the lake,
Jackdaws clustered to drying oils of night in mars-black and nickel.
In the clouds – it was a face I did not know.

Remembering to forget,
It will be evening all afternoon
Forming a Prussian blue line between sea and sky.

From a brief end of days
Swans at Vitznau drew sunlit wakes
In bright silhouettes of what we might have found.

Out of winter's tryptic,
It was your face that I did not know –
Black and white panels of passing lives,
And some end of days in drying oils of night –
Remembering to forget.

Ten Views of a Moment
<for Wallace Stevens>

I
In plain view,
All morning,
Islands did and did not exist.

II
Without permission,
Fires on the beach
Summoned sparks of surrogate stars.

III
The ear of moon
Offered a conch shell tide
In white whisper of oceans all night.

IV
Yellow torches of Siberian iris
Held a premonition of autumn light.

V
Fog covered a canvas of linen fields
In almond flowers and nepenthe of resigned lives.

VI
In a blue veil of hills,
There was likely no path to dawn.
So what.

VII
From Patinas of bronze light,
Monastery bells transmigrated to requiems of grazing herds.

VIII
Under a dusk of harvested skies,
Without judgment,
Ravens brought strokes of woodsmoke
In negative space of sumi-e wings.

IX
Past and present do not end,
As morning and evening mirror the Janus face.
What year do most scholars think it might be?

X
In plain view,
All morning –
Everything did and did not happened.

Tenebrae

At Annabichl gardens,
Without forgiveness,
Stone angels knelt over small boxwoods.

At your final hour,
I sat on a curb in Waco Texas discussing German poets,
Not noticing all the surrounding shadows,
Or luminous choirs of finished light flooding the empty street.

Clouds covered a suicide of liminal stars,
Where words for the beloved became too faint to hear.

A rustling light to the east was only a false lead.

A depressant of night
Completed a sequence beyond our ability to focus or return.

It was not just sunset's old vesper -
It was also channeled lights of Sant'Eugenio,
And distant whispers of traffic in fountains from Giardino delle Cascate.
It was a life's short decay in unfinished histories,
Bleeding white noise of poems.

Stone angels knelt over small boxwoods.

To be loved is rare,
But is of no lasting significance -
And without any desired forgiveness,
I know we are not near,
And cannot hear your voice.

Terrace

In the darkness,
Apricot blossoms rained all night.

Beyond this terrace of an old world,
A lighthouse circled in forensics of cut stars.

At the end of scripted lives,
We waited without expectation overlooking city lights -
Knowing our minor revelations would come again,
And seem new.

In the darkness,
I recalled votives at Abbazia di Santi Severo e Martirio
Holding empty years of tired fire,
Like a rain of apricot blossoms –
Like empty expectation of city lights,
Burning for scripted lives -
With no medics on the way.

Theater of Man

It was too cold to walk on the circling streets.
Orion flared overhead
In quiet alarms of a long count.

As doppelgangers,
We could never find an exit from this ancient house,
Disturbed by found-sounds of slow ghosts,
And pale processions of pyrite stars,
Scraping worn heavens all night.

One does not sleep well in such a space.

From a spasm of night,
Red winds came out of returning days -
Forming the theater of man.

At the altar,
The dead counted burned-out votives in their collected mistakes -
It was a requiem of stalled shadows,
And flicker of too many empty worlds without explanation.

Above circling streets -
Orion flared in quiet alarms,
And for some remaining time,
Red winds came in a long count,
Where, overhead a litany of finished heavens burned in tired fire.
It was a spasm of night and collected cold streets,
With no exit from this house -
Forming the theater of man.

Three Figures at Blue Mesa

In a catalepsy of failing light,
Three figures stood at the edge of the mesa.
It could have been charcoal silhouettes of winter trees.

In what remained of the day,
Exhausted skies sketched disputed histories above a redacted world.

Overhead,
Ashen constellations formed fiery symbols,
Where everything remained hidden by small emergences of the day -
Blocking our return.

Out in the judgment of darkening fields,
A pulse of crickets slowed,
As an irato of crows inked landscapes under alien heavens.

And with truth and faith finally out of reach,
Three figures stood at the edge of the mesa.
It was a catalepsy of failing light -
Black pennons unmoved by the night wind.

It was probably just a specter of woodsmoke,
Or a charcoal sketch of winter trees,
Finishing silhouettes of a redacted world.

Three Trios

"...Sudden in a shaft of light...
...Even while the dust moves...
...Now, here, always..."

- T. S. Eliot

Chamber of Eternity

I

After time's long reign of color -
Darkness, and the drained pool of the day.

In a voice of torches,
Wind flickered over the gray garden:
      hands of air, stroking miles of smoldered leaves.
      It was before and after some static time
      unable to reach '*now*'.

Around us in the autumn light,
It was only fall past or fall future —
Monochromes of red and gold —
      where dark birds cried "*now, now*" -
But only from a re-creation of days,
      and never in the actual moment among these fainting cascades.

Tonight, under the moon's deceptive light,
Half our lives are over — and you said it was good.
We are at ease to be half dead among the flickered ivory of lunar streets.
In the coming realization of half-lives,
Phantoms from time future or remembrances from time past
      crowd-out this ending mirage of the soul's dead zodiac -
      And it was good.

Half-lives –
A limited infinity -
A sweet pathos of afternoon eroded a not yet recalled moment –
Glowing frescoes of recurring seasons,
Circling like coded stars –
Circling like a glittered expanse of ghosts rippling up from the drained
    pool,
Lost in a wave of some next staged event –
This void of the present
and inaccessible time.

At the cathedral,
Across a reanimation of evening,
Candled choirs whispered for the dead
In a syntax void of purpose -
    Cantos lost in a Sargasso Sea of circling 'call and response'.

It became an oppression of clocks,
Where the moment was eternally still-born –
Yet, vitally alive before and after:
Equations of anonymity - A prehistory of integers
A proof in no real numbers,
    and arrows of imaginary time.

Beyond the illusion of our speech -
Beyond this endless trick of afternoon light,
A completed eternity followed us into the garden like a stalker –
    like false histories –
Like our graphic years spent in dreams:
Like darkness,
And the drained pool of the day.

II

Nearer the end,

A presumed map of expanding stars
Surrounded the burned-out crest of our few nights -
A murmur of non-translating futures
Plotted a garden path in coordinates of uncertainty -
Coming in bright white light
    at the predicted hour of death.

Yes, in the sprawl of too many worlds –
Yes, in the violet dusk –
Yes, in the terrain of vacant streets –
Yes, in the rose ticking on the funeral urn of the beloved –
These all say *"now,"*
    beyond our arrival and leaving,
But in a time that was (*or that will be*).
It was a cusp of luminescence,
This endless waking to twilight and thunder over distant mountains:
Lives all unreal.

If all worlds are eternally completed,
Then (*it is true that*) time is already redeemed (*or damned*).
I stretched out my hand for a final singing bird of night,
And the cold fragrance of more than one world –
    of more than one time –
    of more, and only one.

Intent betrays action -
As our words together in the garden
Once echoed to a violence of poems:
Shadows of what seemed like warmth before returning ages of ice.

The glacial sound of evening advanced from the ending summer:
Now - do you hear it? –
Here - ticking footsteps of the condemned on some bridge of sighs –
Always - figures out in the dark –
This disarray of recursive moments:
Terrible dreams of waking to nothing

In a trick of afternoon light.

"*Now now*", but it is already past – (*or yet to be*):
"*Now now*", black equations of time and space,
and the cut maps of our hands.

Nearer the end,
Our silhouettes rippled across a drained pool
Where all worlds were complete.

Skies darkened,
And I stretched out my hand.

III

All times at once.
All worlds at once –
Half our lives – long over, and eventually to begin –
Released histories calculating what will remain,
Among the small tragedies of the day.

Out of these imagined sequences of what is called 'time' –
Out of these snow-calmed streets,
We drifted in a white paralysis,
      the next thought always from memory –
      qbit chants calculating a rehearsed life
But, only from days future (*or nights past*),
      where we stood before crumbled icons
      in the house of our fathers.

It is only forever:
These images coded of Deja vu –
These rotting ghosts of purpose
Running in the echoes of children through spiral summers.
It was a small sacrilege of physics – a corridor of no time –

An illusion of entangled unity,
      held in a dust of what had already happened -
This trivial matter of perception,
As nights came like pages in a book.
And I forever saw you holding a wet poppy from the summer garden.

At the ossuary,
Stone angels grieved for simulated worlds –
It was a background radiation of requiems,
Beyond the day's scripted sequence -
Empty landscapes filling a limit of dreams
For those who are called 'the living'.

"*Now*", all things at once –
"*Now*" our half lives –
      where the world's clamor ends as it begins.

It is only forever,
Some completed spin of seasons –
Some heavens curling over our intended shadows
In a talisman of silver thorns and artificial light,
Yet it is the same glow –
      that comes back from time future (*like time past*) –
      that may yet count some few accomplishments of
      the never-passing day.

It is only forever -
Stylized seasons and a shutter of doves over the zocalo's empty fountain –
Time's long reign of color,
      and this simple mass of night.

We walked cloned harvest fields,
In clockwork-footsteps of scythes,
Hearing winds sweep seas of white wheat -

But it was only a trick of afternoon light -
Ghosts from before and after whispering of 'now'.

Here - it is always the third that follows:
Two shadows drifting through codas of darkening hours,
      with another suspended just beyond the day's slow fingers.

Around us in the autumn light,
It is only now (*forever*) – a vast misunderstanding
      and a thinning glow of halcyon days.

Nearer the end,
Let me show you a clone of the soul's mirage.
Let me show you a monument to uncertainty.
Let me show you purpose in a handful of completed eternities.

After time's long reign of color:
It is this trivial matter of perception -
Darkness, and the drained pool of the day.

Sibyls

I

There are no prophecies within static time,
Where without sequence,
Bells became a voice of the autumn night
As fires brought back our winter:
All things at once,
And nothing.

Along a loop of days -
Space and time became complete -
Hours out of time in a vignette of bokeh skies,
Where in the moment we might have animated a difference.

Approaching now, a pale memory was released.
Perhaps it was Alpen horns above the Bernese Oberland in late summer –
Completing a Dal sago
Where outcomes could only be changed from the beginning (*or the end*).

You said it was some temporal entanglement -
Some superposition merging life and death,
But it was not that simple.
It was a premonition of always and never having been here –
A memory of stepping out to the first snow,
To a returning cold,
Without tyrannies of sequence.

Years ago,
The children of the borough devised a game,
Where everything they witnessed became a staged set –
Lit only as far as they could see:
The old garden as their posed landscape
For all that was perfect and unreal.

At the end's beginning,
We recalled hearing cyclical whispers from the coast -
It was an afternoon of nothing special – a trick of light - the
     beginning's end -
As jade flames of cryptomerias murmured something like our names.
It was nothing personal.

In non-linear evenings,
An abstract palette of faces appeared at steamed windows:
And empty streets filled with ravens and black flight of campanile bells,
Bringing inhuman shadows - reflections, not our own -
A perpetual time like the death rattle of bare trees at evening,
After and before a cold sleep's white moment.

From all these redacted memories,
From our never-finished fifth act,

Around us in the Autumn light -
It was a held breath under the drained pool's blue asphyxiation.

All things at once -
A pendulum of clocks in the sound of dragging feet —
Circular histories closing a worn loop of what is called time.
The more we observed, colors because less rich.
The more we listened, voices become less clear.
It was nothing personal.

Above the cathedral,
There was a flight of carbon stars -
It was a hiss of votive fire for the departed and the yet unborn.

Here in the mirror with faces not our own,
We became surrogates for the living:
Unattended marionettes in a shadowbox dropped from careless hands.

Between the intent and action -
Between the living and graven images of the living -
Between the observer and the observed -
It was a collapse of uncertainly into all this unredeemed *(or damned)*
    space.

Out of the house of our fathers,
It will be entangled histories written in cloud-chambers all night.
It will be the breathing of things that do not breath like living men —
A script of winter ghosts bringing a simulation and a rest:
Echoes of voices that can never speak directly for themselves.

Here, in the cut map of our hands - Here, finding time laid-out like space —
As bells became a voice of the autumn night —
Where a troubled duality of certainty and premonition remain.
Voices came from after *(or before)* in faint preces of call and response,
As memories of the cold will come again —
In a momentary eternity and pentimento of a girl's face I would have
    recalled.

Years ago, at Jupiter's temple on Capitoline hill,
The remaining Sibylline books could not have foreseen everything had already happened.
There were shadows on the wall,
But no one could awake.
There were old futures circling the past -
As our attempted words in the garden
Strained to cross some small Boötes void between us -
Avatars in the wings of the stage -
All things at once,
And nothing.

II

From our graphic years in dreams –
Beyond these sad landscapes in pixels -
And the lovely Planck-length of afternoon -
Everything was long-competed and yet to occur.

From a slurred speech of waves along the coast,
It seemed a recall of lives past,
But it was only the held breath of what we could not say:
Sepia prints of smiling faces in the garden without essence –
A regret of simulations across too many entangled lives -
Long finished and always about to begin.

Under this litany of ersatz worlds –
It was an altered sequence of remembering –
And calculations of replayed days.
It was nothing personal.

Around us in the Autumn light,
Let me show you some few moments that can never pass.
Let me show you a sad landscape that cannot be changed:
Now - as time is laid-out like space:

Here – with histories losing color after and before the fixed moment:
Always – illusions born in the intent of looking, or the looking away.

III

As we returned,
Nearer the end,
A superposition of sleep and waking continued without our consent,
But it was not that simple.

Now - For a few moments of forever,
It was a staged perception of remaining color and old age,
With nothing left but a return of all our undesired many worlds.

Here - All night - crowds did and did not pass along the vacant brumal
    streets:
Lame prophecies from before or after,
Saying we can never decide when it is time.

Always - Beyond some base reality,
The moment unraveled into a double slit of dusk and dawn –
Fusing fact and possibility in the long wait for 'now'.

From a small expanse of recorded time -
Out of this block universe,
I have seen our shadows walking apart from us
Where the darkened garden became unfamiliar:
A child's game of endless simulations beyond what could be seen.

The cold will come again,
And dust of the beloved will move through completed seasons,
Where old dualities of light will continue to suspend our disbelief
Across this flickered trick of afternoon.

Nearer the end,
It will be a movement without sequence –

Bells becoming a voice of the autumn night,
As fires brought back our winter.

Wood of the Ladder

I

From this winter house,
We awoke in the hypnagogic half-light,
You held a last poppy from the summer garden -
It became a red shift of receding fire
And blossoming opiate under indole-ring skies.

In the casual looking or looking-away,
Where we remained both dead and alive (*in time past or time future*),
Our silhouettes startled to a delayed choice -
It was a catecholamine waking to more than one world,
Where illusion climbed the wood of the ladder to morning's false glow.

It was a premonition of no free will -
It was the recalled scent of the beloved's wet hair -
It was the callous replay of the static day:
Lives all unreal.

It will come that the many only entangle to one,
As our talks in the garden became merely recited lines -
Doppelgangers that do not throw umbrages like living men -
Premonitions of yesterday, and futures long finished.

Now - Outside careful landscapes of base reality.
Here - From elaborate histories written in ghosts.
Always - Vapor drawings of what we might have accomplished
     from our graphic years spent in dreams and acetylcholine prayers.

From this winter house,
Storms came in black horses woven of wind,
And clotted crows surrounding a mortal wound of all that was to come.
It was qbits of unresolved music at the predicted hour of death.
It was the hypnogogic half-light,
Counting days as numbered steps back to the beginning.
We remembered the scent of October fires.
We remembered being young,
But it was not that simple,
Here at the end of summer and simulations across too many worlds.

In this long exhale,
In a before and after of what we had intended to do,
It will come that all choices have been made -
Premonitions of yesterday,
Where the cold will come again,
And you will continue to hold a last poppy from the summer garden.

II

Coming to the place of small hours,
The voices called *"Follow us into the garden past the drained pool"*.
Unreal landscapes fell in remembered details around our feet,
Where an infinite moment of bad dreams continued.

Between recitatives of memories,
And debris of before and after,
We stood still with little chance to awake -
    it was murals of birds giving the perception of flight
    where there is only a frieze without motion.

From what has long happened and may yet begin again,
A scripted evening arrived.

Here, with no forgiveness,
Everything was becoming complete and unfinished.
We knew the nimbus of light was never real -
A halo around the hanged man –
A children's game in some ever-twilight,
Suspended in hidden variables of catalogued heavens -
A surrender to stillness that seemed like motion,
And silence that seemed like sound.

The voices called: *"Follow us into the garden"* –
"Follow us into seasons that do not pass" –
"Follow us into years spent in dreams" -
"Follows us into the turning point of the still world" -
More real in reflections of the drained pool.

Beyond the garden gate,
It was a transcendence of refusing to witness the moment,
Keeping humanity from too much unreality –
Here at the turning point –
Here at the clear promise of uncertainty –
Here at the place of small hours,
Here, where a moment of bad dreams could only continue.

III

As we returned,
It was a last glow in reflections from the eye's drained pool.

We have heard the prophecy of birds
Saying *'Now – Now'* -
Carving dark glyphs against completed indole-ring skies,
But it was only the inhale and exhale of our exhausted light,
Entangling dreams without a dreamer.

As we returned,

A child came along the empty hallway not yet afraid of the expanding night,
Or the gnarled figures waiting out in staged autumn streets:
It was only reflections in the mirror of faces not our own.

Somewhere between after-before and before-after,
It will be a remembered forgetting of days –
An expanse of free will without choice -
A double slit of dusk and dawn,
And the unreal embrace of a lover in the Planck length of afternoon.

All times at once –
All worlds at once.
Here between the calculation and the result -
Between the wave and particle –
Between the looking and the looking away -
It was only an endless trick of afternoon light,
Suggesting that morning might yet come.
It was a resolution of our many worlds collapsing to 'now'.

Around us in the Autumn light,
One evening we came out to a cured-gold of falling leaves –
It was an October glow fostering a selfless senescence,
It was this void of the present and inaccessible time –
A limited infinity,
Where all returning hours could only be anticipated or recalled.

Without sequence,
You said half our lives were over –
As voices continued calling us into illusions of the garden.

Nearer the end
It will be time's long reign of color.
It will be dark birds crying: *'Now – Now'*
As fires brought back our winter,
Where the cold will come again.

Now – Let me show you the end as a beginning.
Here – Let me show you purpose at the turning point of the still world.
Always – Let me show you all times at once - And it was good.

Τώρα, Εδώ, Πάν

Three Views of the Evening

I

The plaza was filled with crows and red light.
Couples walked arm in arm with mescal cups,
Under a low marigold sun.

Streets became rivers of sandalwood and shadows,
Where children with wooden puppets staged a tragic scene.

By the cathedral,
Lovely graves were decorated with candles, amaranth seeds and honey,
Leading a slow procession to night.

In these high villages before winter,
Our fate was well placed in the wind's hands,
As cicadas spoke liturgies under golden leaves of an ancient sun.

From this ledge of blooming stars –
All summer, it was fall.
Among dark torches of cryptomerias,
Mountains tilted over a falling arc of the lark,
And hard clay roads followed into a remote time.

Bells came over Santuario de Las Lajas
In soft voices of grey and white terns -
It was only a premonition of what time might remain.

From the beginning -
With no destination,
We watched the light fade in the cry of every bird.

II

It cannot be changed,
This caravan of dusk –

This rosary of completed heavens
Stalling over clasped hands.

Under autumn elms
Our ancestors rocked in a swollen boat of night.

It was a time where we could no longer focus –
A caesura in the mind –
Eternity arriving on the finite wheel of stopped clocks.

It cannot be changed,
This human myth –
This fallen summer of luminous youth
Held in the nerve's yellow torch -
This uncertain glitter of the atom -
This drunken flame of multiple worlds -
This elegant end.

Still calculations of twilight came back over a reddening canyon,
Painting our faces with an aging 'now'.
In the closing streets,
There was a dust of chrysanthemums
Littering histories in fallen gold –
As we watched the light fade in the cry of every bird.

III

Filling dusk's chiaro cup –
Skies turned to shades of mountain snow:
Keppel prints of ocean in verdigris slate and dry herbs: Residual
images covering more than one life.

From the beginning,
We were silhouettes made of fire and ash,
Where nothing could be changed.

Under a low marigold sun,
With no destination,
Our fate was well placed in the wind's hands,
Where from a ledge of blooming stars –
All summer it was fall,
And we watched the light fade in the cry of every bird.

To a Minor 21ˢᵗ Century Poet

As little as you finished,
Your eigenstate of poems yet occasionally collapsed to now.

Trust blinded the Buddhas,
Where finding eternity was easy,
Yet holding the moment was hard.

Perhaps you saw,
It was only to reach across all this darkness,
In a superposition of words
That occasionally collapsed to now.

Traveling in the Mountains
<for Tu Mu>

Skies brighten after evening snow.

Last sumacs and maples coursed down the canyon
In panling lanshan robes of impermanent red.

After official duties –
I have come to this terrace of clouds
To lose what was found over many years -
And let go what might yet remain.

Tuscan Dusk

From an eroded terrace of stone and thunder,
Pennons of Oleanders sailed in a linen wind.
Not everyone could return.

We walked in shadows under Tuscan olives –
Where bells and terns counted jade hours
Over ascending cressets of cypress flames.

Carved doves rested on exedras,
And vineyards flowed across a gauze of hills
Like tended lawns for cenotaphs.

Evening arrived in a recalled light,
Piecing together urns of soft fire
In clouds for the forgotten.

Bells and terns counted jade hours.
All our worlds were not perfect.
Not everyone could return.

Union Station – 10 p.m.

Wet streets closed the blurred summer,
Bringing a night of ghosts to the Oxford hotel.

On a wooden bench outside Union station,
I thought I saw Trakl and Tranströmer
Reading Ingeborg Bachmann -
Unaware of each other.

Valle di Cadore
<at Casa Galeazzi del Carmine>

Without warning,
Dusk released a wild ravine
In blue fire of swollen grapes.

Preparing for fall -
A parchment of stars became inked with nightshade of crows.

Votives were being lit at la Chiesa di San Rocco with care,
For no one.

Vespers

Vespers of wind came around the convent
Bringing voices of November.

The sisters came across snow-lit cloisters
Burning small sticks of styrax and copal
Under stone arches of saints and daemons.

Cloud-Trikirons holding ocher stars became extinguished
From a gathered darkness in the olive grove.

All night in rescinded permissions,
Ghosts waited under a white rattle of weeping birch trees
Where icy constellations
Offered pale blankets for the dead.

When it is Time

When it is time –
Bright afternoons will come up from an unexpected end of days.

When it is time –
Cerement clouds will wrap expanding larimar skies
In siren voices of oceanwind,
With drafts of pieces we could not complete.

It will be the faint sound of autumn leaves out in the garden -
A stone glancing off inked lines of black bamboo –
Some short promise of youth,
And the death-rattle of love.

It will be a bright, unfinished afternoon -
A simple unexpected enlightenment,
And expanding skies –
It will not be important,
When it is time.

Whispered in the Evening

Whispered in the evening,
Your voice receded in quiet fire of Jacarandas.

Above azure waters,
Ravens pieced together a darkness of October,
Mapping light years of a futile sleep.

Under jasmine and olibanum skies,
Violet clouds of dusk
Carried your boat of exile
Over the dream's plagiarized passage.

You will die again in Greece.
Our hours will return,
And cascades of autumn crocus
Will weep all night along the Plaka.

Stars in clusters of fatal pink colchicums
Burned over carbon-dated texts of your lost words.
It was a future that was always past.

Whispered in the evening,
It was waiting in a long silence of failing color -
It was a short space of resounding years -
It was what remained,
As your voice receded to silence under quiet fire of Jacarandas.

Winter Garden

Passing by,
The evening could never be attained.

A golden tiara of clematis encircled your hair.
Far across the completed afternoon
White winds spoke our names.

An early moon made tracks in a first snow
Where few could follow.

Our lamps were dimming,
And papers of unfinished poems littered this small room,
As the winter evening continued for no one in particular.

In a last untranslated phrase of color,
Perhaps we walked in the garden once more
With all we have desired -
But our lamps were out of oil,
And there was the issue of the ever-approaching moment
That could never be attained.

Winter Morning

As crows calculated dark strokes of pointillist clouds,
Another morning came.

In the cold,
There were Bonnard brushes of pallid trees
And 'Les Nabis' blurs of still snow.
Perhaps it was a hiss of hot water for tea,
Or steamed-over windows of the vertigo day -
Absent a sun wrapped in worn blankets of December.

Perhaps it was the silence of distant fields,
With ice of fallen leaves reflecting a final corundum of hills,
But for a moment in the gilded grey glow,
I thought you were still here.

Zen and Chan Redux

As it was faithfully reported,
At the faint knock of a discarded pebble glancing off bamboo,
Hsiang-yen shattered the uncountable worlds -
Yet old Musō Soseki simply by letting his white hair fall free,
Brought them all back together.

About the Author

Stan K. Yeatts writes under the monogram - S. K. Yeatts and holds a BA in English Literature from Baylor University in Texas. He formerly served as the Executive Director for a Fortune 50 Company leading UX design teams and software development. He now works full time on art and literary projects and lives with his wife Janette in the Sangre de Cristo mountains above Santa Fe, New Mexico – US.

Yeatts is both a poet and a visual artist. His initial collection of poetry – "**HOLOGLYPHS –** *Twilight Fields*" was published by Kelsay Books in 2016 and won the Independent Press Award, the Pinnacle Book Achievement Award, the Big New York Book Award 'Distinguished Favorite' selection and was the winner of the 2019 Next Generation Indie Book Award for Poetry.

His literary work has drawn comparisons to T. S. Eliot, Po Chü-I, Robert Bly, James Wright, and Friedrich Hölderlin, as his poetry emerges at the intersection of tradition, and experimentation.

Yeatts' poetic direction aligns with the term - 'Hologlyph'. Hologlyph is a neologism, fused from the terms 'whole' and 'image', and describes a poetic style centered in imagistic archetypes – aspiring to Ezra Pound's vision of the "Luminous detail".

Akin to his poetry, Yeatts' visual art focuses on extracting the archetypal nature of an image by working in a unique blend of photography and graphics he refers to as *"Post-Photographic Impressionism"*. His work spans the polarities of designing album covers for US & European musicians to creating large- format panoramas for residential and commercial installations. Yeatts has exhibited his pieces in international juried photographic shows in North America and Western Europe, including an invitation to show at the recent 4th Biennial of Fine Art & Documentary Photography Expose' in Berlin Germany.